LIFE ALONG THE

APALACHICOLA RIVER

JIM MCCLELLAN

THE
History
PRESS

Published by The History Press
Charleston, SC 29403
www.historypress.net

Copyright © 2014 by Jim McClellan
All rights reserved

First published 2014
Second printing 2014

ISBN 978-1-5402-1208-5

Library of Congress Control Number: 2014953165

For my father, Gene McClellan, who taught me to love and appreciate the outdoors, and my mother, Betty, who insisted on Sunday school, good manners, proper grammar and taking my boots off outside; for my brothers, Mack, Hentz, Steve and Bill, who are at various times mentors and tormentors, teachers and critics, shining examples and cautionary tales; for my long-suffering wife, Mary, who has been at my side with love and patience through the high times and the bitter lows; and for my children, Mary Grace, Ella and Jimmy, who helped me understand why preserving these stories and memories is so important.

CONTENTS

PREFACE

About forty-five miles due west of Tallahassee, Florida State Road 20 leaves the high bluffs of Liberty County, crosses the wide, green-brown Apalachicola River and gradually descends into the floodplains along its west bank. You're in Calhoun County now and entering my hometown of Blountstown, a community that developed adjacent to and because of the river.

The Apalachicola is formed from the confluence of the Flint and Chattahoochee Rivers, which meet at Lake Seminole on the Georgia border, just above the Jim Woodruff Dam. From there, it twists and bends southward one hundred miles or so to the coast.

Locals call it the "Big River" to distinguish it from the Chipola, its smaller, clearer tributary. The Chipola originates in Jackson County, cuts through the western side of Calhoun County and meanders southeasterly through the Dead Lakes in Gulf County, where it meets up with the Apalachicola near Wewahitchka. This boost from the Chipola helps the river feed the large, productive Apalachicola Bay estuary—a nursery for countless species of fish, oysters, shrimp and other sea life.

Along the Apalachicola's eastern bank are Gadsden and Liberty Counties, with Franklin occupying both banks at the Bay. These counties, in turn, are bordered to their east by the Ochlocknee system, which feeds Apalachee Bay.

With much of its area cradled by the three rivers, the region has long been a haven for people who made their livings and their lives in the great outdoors. With all the farmers, loggers, hunters and fishermen in the area, you'd be hard-pressed to find a soul who isn't connected to the woods and water in some way. And that's reflected in the culture and in the spirit of the people who call this area home.

Those of us who grew up along the Apalachicola River—in places like Blountstown, Bristol and a dozen similar small towns—enjoy a special relationship with it. No one can "own" a river, but all of us feel like the Apalachicola is ours. We fish in its channels and under the willows on its banks. We hunt the ridges and cypress hammocks along its edges. We swim in it, ski on it and sometimes drink from it.

For several generations of my family and many others, it has been a source of recreation, occupation, occasional frustration and frequent inspiration. The Apalachicola belongs to us, and we belong to it.

Like many of my friends and family members, I'm worried now that we're losing it. We're losing the river to mismanagement and drought. We're losing our lifestyle to growth and development. We're losing the people, the stories and the experiences. And if we're not careful, we'll lose our very identity as well. That would be a shame.

Writing these stories is like paddling upstream, into the past, hoping to capture and preserve pieces of it before the current pushes me away. I want to share my memories with our children and their children. I want them to meet in print the characters they couldn't know in person. Mostly, I want to save them from being fully absorbed into a generic world, filled with plastic, soulless, disconnected people.

They deserve better. They deserve to hear the outrageous stories, share in the laughter and appreciate the grit, guts and gall that defined the generations whose paths they can still follow through that river swamp.

In the pages ahead, I've put to paper just a handful of the many, many stories and thoughts that shaped my life from childhood to the present day. They've made me laugh, curse, scratch my head and occasionally shed a tear. But mostly they've given me a deep appreciation for my upbringing on and around the Apalachicola River.

I just hope I've done them justice in the telling.

ACKNOWLEDGEMENTS

R eaders should understand that I was reared in a virtual cocoon of loving family and friends in Blountstown, Florida. Parents and grandparents, brothers and cousins, aunts and uncles surrounded me with love and affection throughout my childhood. Family friends and neighbors, many of whom I addressed as uncles and aunts, were always there to protect me, guide me and hold me accountable for any misbehavior.

I count myself lucky to have had Grandmother Hentz; Daddy Mac and Mother Mac; Uncle Billy and Aunt Ann; Aunt Annette; Uncle Jim and Aunt Harriett; Aunt Elna; Aunt Eloise; my favorite in-laws, Fred and Susie Donovan; my "shirttail buddy" Charlie Cook Bridges; and Mrs. Mary Cathryn. There were Frank and Mildred Guilford, Jackie and Marie Simpson, Owen and Jo House, Cheryl and Tootie Wood, Gary and Susan Purvis and so many more. The real story behind this book starts there, but to make it complete would take several volumes. Instead, let me start with the people who were there with me from the origins of this book, when it was in blog form.

First, I flat-out copied the idea from my friend Kent Koptiuch, whose stories of life in the outdoors could fill several books—and those are just the ones he can talk about. Wyette Donovan convinced me to pour my restless spirit into writing, while Meg Andronaco offered some very important early encouragement.

It was my friend, mentor and brother in spirit, Ron Sachs, who guided much of my career and who taught me to write with passion and purpose.

Then there was my original editor: fellow Guardsman, former Marine and editorial page editor Lloyd Brown, who whipped the early version of the blog into shape. Thanks, too, to my brother Steve, who caught every typo, misspelling or awkwardly worded sentence without fail.

Author, poet and editor Alison Trotta's courage and practical advice helped me through my initial jitters. Through Ali, I met Blake Richardson Leyers, whose father was a wildlife officer and who helped me realize that my stories could resonate beyond a local audience.

My brother Bill plays a central role in many of my stories, though he also served as a technical consultant, frequent reality checker and partner in crime.

Inexplicably, my brother Hentz continues to allow me to use his boat when I'm in Blountstown, while also keeping me updated on current events around the area. He and my oldest brother, Mack, also provide some much-needed historical perspective and memory checks for me.

I also want to thank the people who contributed so many wonderful photographs for the book: my great friend Maria Rogers Heil; Chris Atkins, my friend and the grandson of legendary Calhoun County educator and historian George Atkins; Matthew Godwin of Off the Map Expeditions; FWC biologist Chris Paxton, who is a terrific resource for Florida; my daughter Ella McClellan; and my good friend, lobbyist and nuisance alligator trapper Lane Stephens. My friend Dana Holway has lent her talents to this project in a number of ways, including photo editing, legal advice and occasional pep talks. And Cliff and Lisa Golden Bristol provided a photo and some great historical information as well.

Teresa Eubanks, editor of the *Calhoun-Liberty Journal*, convinced me that my blog posts would make a good column for her weekly paper. I had my doubts, but she has stayed after me and we've managed to keep them going for more than two years now. Teresa even sent photographer Domenick Esgro to accompany me for a day and evening in the swamp. We got some great pictures, and I repaid her by bringing him home alive.

I want to say a special thanks to Hayes Leonard, the heart and soul of Iamonia Lake Hunting and Fishing Club. His commitment and patience have preserved the club and are restoring its magic. I also want to thank all the members of that club, past and present—especially Tommy Williams and Billy Stoutamire—for keeping the memories alive and for ensuring that it's a place where I always feel at home. Thanks also to Tim Jenks, whose energy and passion are making it even better.

Finally, I need to say thanks to my friend and former boss Phil McMillan and the folks at Neal Land & Timber Company. Much of our region's history is intertwined with Neal's, and the company played an important role in its development. Neal also owns the land where we hunt, and I'm deeply indebted to it for allowing us that privilege.

INTRODUCTION

Have you ever gigged a frog on a riverbank? Shot a blackfish off a trotline? Dug the "pearls" out of a catfish head? Picked up scallops in St. Joe Bay? Prayed for the resurrection of an illegal fish?

It doesn't matter, really. If you have, then maybe these stories will jar loose some memories you can share with others. God knows, all of us who grew up between Chattahoochee and Apalachicola ought to have plenty of them.

But even if you believe that the great outdoors is the space between your front door and the car door, these stories might prompt you to leave the television and the computer and pick up a pole or a shotgun. (Or they might just make you a bit more thankful for the roof over your head and the grocery store down the street.) Spend a little while with me in the pages ahead, and you'll get a sense for what it was like to hunt and fish in the sprawling Apalachicola River swamp in days gone by and hopefully understand why it remains so important to our way of life today.

Forget about the caricatures you see so often in modern media. In this book, you'll meet the real-life characters: genuine outdoors folks, some of whom are still among us and some of whom live on within us.

This book includes quite a bit of history, but it's not intended to be a definitive source for dates and events. Thanks to the Internet and a world of other resources, the official records of a place are much easier now to access, preserve and present. Likewise, the deeds of the famous and the infamous tend to be well documented for posterity.

INTRODUCTION

What time erodes more than anything are the stories of the real people who bring that history to life. To me, nothing reveals as much about a region as a glimpse into the lives of ordinary folks, their surroundings and how they've adapted to their circumstances.

For the people who live along the Apalachicola River, our lives have been shaped and carved by the flowing water and all that it provides. It has drawn us to a life out of doors, pursuing fun and food in its forests for as long as people have inhabited this area.

Understanding the region means understanding the river and the culture it has spawned. And to my way of thinking, there's no better way to present that culture than through humor. Much of the backwoods wisdom that has been passed down through the ages in our area has traveled in the form of funny stories and insights. Jesus often taught through parables. Our folks taught with laughter.

Let me add that these stories are as true and real as I can remember them—or remember hearing them, as the case may be. Most involve my friends, my family members or me, but readers familiar with the area and its inhabitants will attest that they are reflective of the entire region. If I offend you on these pages, then you probably deserve it. And if you think I've gotten anything wrong, well, you can fix it when you write your own book.

Enjoy.

Part I

SHALL WE GATHER AT THE RIVER?

"Shall We Gather at the River?" is an old hymn that remains in frequent rotation at churches throughout Northwest Florida. The hymn uses the titular river as a symbol of heaven, with saints and the faithful assembled there. I always enjoyed it because it spoke to me on a more literal level as well.

Most every Sunday would find my mother, Betty, worshiping in the Blountstown United Methodist Church, while my father honored the Sabbath in his own sanctuaries, deep in the woods or out on the water. So, while she was singing the hymn's central question from the church pews, he was often answering in the affirmative from the seat of his boat. Mama once asked him, "Gene, what are you going to tell the Good Lord when he asks you why you missed so much church?" According to her, his response was, "I'll just tell him that I sure did enjoy his creation." Mama intended to be on the banks of that river one day. Daddy didn't want to wait.

The truth is that all of us, including my mother, were always drawn to the water and the outdoors. The best memories from my childhood are from times spent on the Apalachicola, at Daddy Mac's camp on the Chipola, down at my father's camp or at dozens of other places on the water's edge.

I think it was the same for our friends and neighbors and most everyone in our little community and others up and down the river. Something inside tells all of us that the river is where we belong. It's where we are meant to gather.

THE IAMONIA LAKE HUNTING AND FISHING CLUB

Of these gathering places, the one that figures prominently in stories throughout this chapter and, indeed, the entire book is Iamonia Lake, an oxbow in the southern part of Calhoun County that was probably the river's main channel eons ago. (By the way, Iamonia Lake should not be confused with Leon County's bigger and more famous Lake Iamonia.)

In 1934, a group of men including my maternal grandfather, J.I. Hentz, formed a hunting and fishing club on the surrounding property that was owned by Neal Lumber Company (now Neal Land and Timber Company).

According to club president Hayes Leonard, his grandfather, Drayton Burke "D.B." Hayes, was the main catalyst behind the club's formation. Mr. Hayes was an employee and part owner of Neal's who was also serving as the mayor of Brewton, Alabama, when he was sent on a "temporary" assignment to Blountstown in the mid-1920s. With a keen mind for business, Mr. Hayes's job was to determine if a mill would be financially viable, but he fell in love with the area and never left, eventually bringing his wife and children as well.

Neal built the mill, harvesting the hardwood trees from the river bottom and providing jobs and income to residents until its closure in the early '70s. Meanwhile, Mr. Hayes developed a great appreciation for all the Apalachicola region had to offer, especially the camaraderie of the Iamonia Lake Club.

According to Mr. Leonard, "My grandfather believed that if he led a good life, he would go to Iamonia Lake when he passed away."

Sometime around 1938, the members of the club built a cabin on a high ridge at the northern end of the lake. Over the years, the Clubhouse has been repainted, remodeled and rewired. There are several generations of add-ons and a lot of furniture that I suspect was rerouted on a trip to the junkyard.

The central feature of the "living room" is a big octagonal poker table that has been there since the mid-1940s. It was built by William "Bill" Bristol, who opened a cabinet shop after returning from World War II. His son, Blountstown physician Cliff Bristol, said that his father and his grandfather, Harold, were part of a "pot club" that regularly played

Iamonia Lake Clubhouse. *Original oil painting by Suzanne Conner.*

poker at the Clubhouse. Its members included Mr. Hayes and his son, Brooks; Jim Ramsey; Allen Stewart; and several others. When the group decided that it needed a "real" table, Harold commissioned his son to do the job.

According to Dr. Bristol, Harold and Bill enjoyed the games so much that the pair once traveled from their home (in Bristol, coincidentally) to the Clubhouse by boat because the local ferry was out of service. That's a long haul even with a modern motor. It must have been an odyssey in those days, but such was the attraction of the game and the company.

Hanging on one wall of the Clubhouse is a framed roster of members from 1984. I'm not sure what was magic about that year, but I'm glad the old document is there. I know almost all the people on it, living and dead, and seeing their names makes it feel like they're all still close by. And if Mr. Hayes was right, maybe they really are.

The other artwork on the walls is a frequent source of commentary as well. I'm sure a lot of the décor was sent from good homes, likely by wives whose parting words were, "Get that tacky thing out of my house right now."

As a result, we have pictures of a grizzly bear, a pheasant, a Brant goose, rainbow trout, brook trout and pink salmon. Know what all of these species have in common? You won't find any of them anywhere near Iamonia Lake. There's also a buck deer leaping over a snowbank and a glass "Bless This Kitchen" prayer for good measure.

For proof of how much the Apalachicola River has declined, look no further than the two boat ramps on the club property: the original one on the creek and the new one on the lake. The latter was built in the '80s, when long periods of low water made the former unusable much of the time.

After my parents passed away, we sold the house where I grew up. Nowadays, the old white Clubhouse is about the last building in Calhoun County where I truly feel like I'm home—where it's okay to walk in unannounced, make a pot of coffee, take a shower, take a nap or clean a mess of fish.

No matter what else has changed through the years, that feeling of home is the same now as it was forty years ago.

THE GATOR WHISPERER

My father was something of a fixture at the Clubhouse, one of the regulars who would often be found cooking fish on a Thursday or Saturday evening. He enjoyed few things as much as fishing, cooking, eating and drinking with his friends. Occasionally, however, visitors or members from out of town would show up, and he made it his business to welcome them…in his own special way.

For example, one afternoon such a group struck up a conversation about alligators and Daddy generously provided an unforgettable lesson for the group. Unfortunately, the real takeaway was why Iamonia Lake is a terrible place to be gullible.

During the course of the conversation, someone mentioned calling alligators. Since baby alligators "chirped" and the mama gators responded, they wondered if humans could do the same thing. At this point, my father weighed in and told them he could call up a gator any time he wanted. In fact, he said he could get one to come right up to the bank of the creek, just a few yards away from where they were sitting. When they asked how, he held his hand to his mouth and yelled in a high-pitched voice, "Heeeere gator, gator, gator!"

The group immediately called BS, but Daddy offered to prove it right then. In a classic put-up-or-shut-up moment, he walked down to the creek bank and started in with his ridiculous call (probably adding a name like "Dixie" or "George" for effect).

Everyone had a big laugh at the spectacle…right up until a six-foot gator appeared in the black water, fifty feet away and swimming directly toward them. When the gator got close, Daddy turned and casually walked back up to the Clubhouse with some newly and duly impressed visitors watching in stunned silence.

Convinced that they had witnessed some backwoods black magic, they asked him how it worked. And Daddy laid it on thick, explaining that it was all about the hand placement, the rhythm and the pitch of his voice. He even had them try it themselves a few times just for good measure (and to prove that only he had the magic touch).

If my father ever told me who those folks were, I've long since forgotten. But I can make a couple of really solid assumptions. For one, I know that they didn't spend much time around the Clubhouse. Otherwise, they would have realized that Daddy called this particular gator only after walking right past the cleaning bench. That was the spot where everyone "recycled" their fish heads and guts into the creek on a daily basis. He was also careful to

Alligator soaking up the sunlight. *Photo by Matthew Godwin, Off the Map Expeditions, LLC.*

step on a piece of tin at the water's edge that made a slight but distinctive splashing sound as he called.

The other thing I know about this group of onlookers is that they clearly didn't know my father well. If they had, they would have recognized the exact moment when they should have become suspicious of a trick. That moment was when he started talking.

HOT SAUCE ON THE HOUSEBOAT

As much as my father enjoyed dishing it out, there were some times when he got a taste of his own medicine. One time in particular, it was with a dose of hot sauce.

My father loved the stuff—the hotter the better. I've always suspected that his taste buds had been fried by gallons of the best pepper concoctions that folks like Mr. Ben Clark and others could come up with. It was a point of pride for Daddy that he could take a swallow of even the most caustic creations and not show any outward signs of discomfort. At the house, we often had two bottles of pepper sauce on the table—one for Daddy and another for everyone else.

In his later years, I asked him if he ever found any hot sauce that he wouldn't try. His response was, "No, but I sure drank some I wish I hadn't." That's when he told me about an ill-fated trip down the river one night to visit Tommy Williams and Sonny Bailey on their houseboat.

The two told him that they were making a batch of hot sauce and invited him to come try some—if he thought he could handle it. There was no way he could let that challenge go unanswered, and Tommy and Sonny knew it. They apparently also knew how to create a weapons-grade pepper sauce because Daddy said when he took a sip, it was all he could do to swallow it.

"That was the hottest stuff I had ever put in my mouth," Daddy said. "My tongue and throat were burning, and I could feel it all the way into my nose." His pride being what it was, Daddy couldn't let on to Tommy and Sonny that it was about to burn his face off. He certainly couldn't get any water or wash his mouth out. So, he had to sit there and act like it was no big deal. (Tommy told me that the most Daddy would admit was that it was "fair to middlin'.")

Daddy said they kept him sitting there talking for what seemed like an eternity. Meanwhile, all he could think about was the six-pack of beer he had on ice

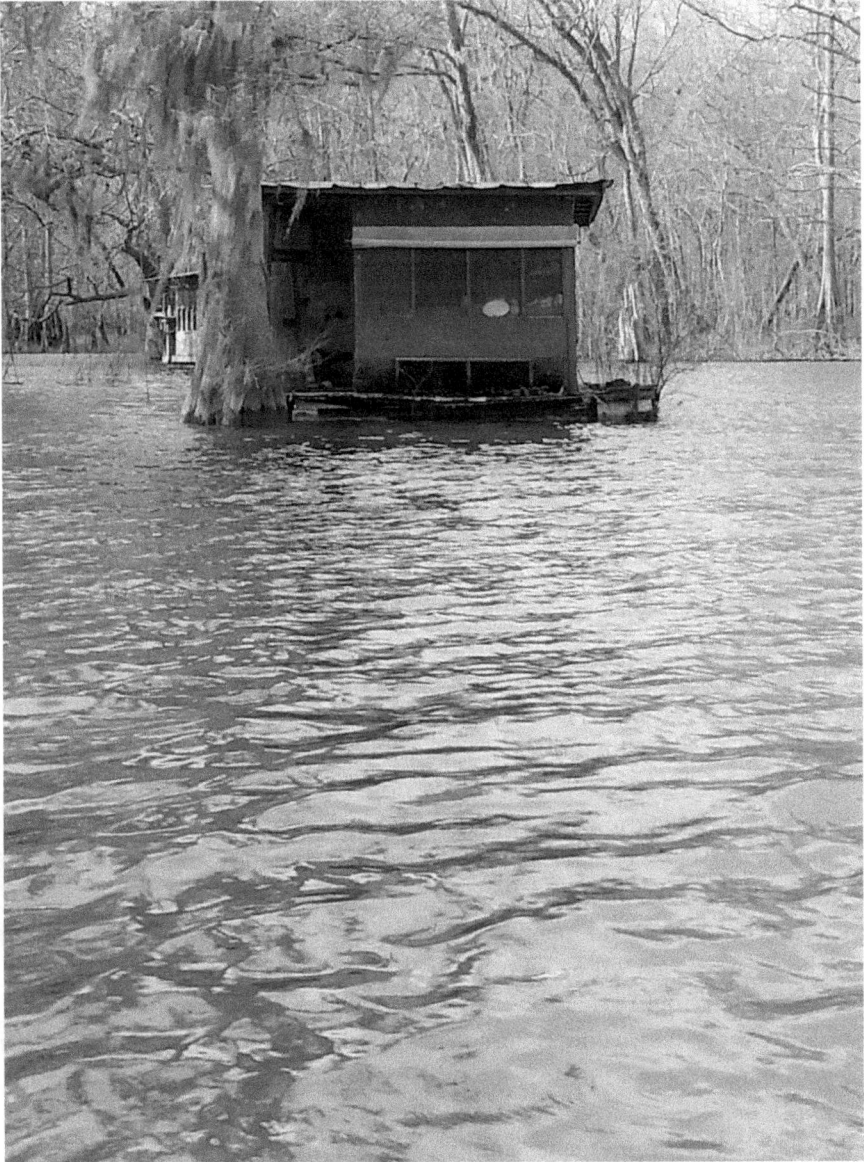

Old houseboat at Iamonia Lake. *Photo by Maria Rogers Heil.*

in his cooler. He knew that once he left, he could get some cold, carbonated comfort. But they kept finding excuses for why he needed to stay and talk.

After a long and painful while, they finally let him say his goodbyes, hop in his boat and take off. Daddy was careful to make it around the bend from the houseboat—well out of sight of Tommy and Sonny—before he allowed himself to open his cooler. But the pair had anticipated that. So when he reached for an ice-cold beer, what he found instead was a whole lot of nothing. At some point, one of his hosts had sneaked out to Daddy's boat, taken the beer from his cooler and dumped out the ice.

I asked Daddy if he went back and got his six-pack. "No, I couldn't do that. But I did lean over the side of the boat and drink a bunch of river water as fast as I could."

Daddy always enjoyed homemade pepper sauce and often brought home a bottle or two someone had given him. But for all the different kinds we had around the house, I don't think any of them came from Tommy and Sonny.

Mary Meets the Camp

As the crow flies, it's about a mile from the Iamonia Lake Clubhouse to my father's camp on the bank of one of the many sloughs that connect the river to the lake. And no matter what someone might think of the Clubhouse, it's the Taj Mahal compared to the camp.

A few days before Thanksgiving in 1990, I suggested to my brand-new bride, Mary, that we spend the holiday down at the camp. I explained that the annual hunting trip was a tradition for some of my brothers and me, and I thought she might enjoy it as well. To my surprise, she agreed and seemed really excited by the idea.

Now, Mary was by no means a woods-person, so I should have suspected that something was wrong right then. But it was only when I mentioned bringing a tent that I realized we were facing a major communications gap. Specifically, we had wildly different ideas about the meaning of the word *camp*. That's because in Mary's world, going to the camp meant staying at her Uncle Sid and Aunt Millicent's summer/weekend home in Pass Christian, Mississippi. Their "camp" was actually a nice brick home that featured multiple bedrooms, central air and a heated pool.

"Why do we need a tent?" she asked. "Aren't we staying in the camp?" The question was as innocent to her as it was ridiculous to me.

"What? You mean *inside* the camp? Oh, no!" I said. My skin crawled just thinking about it. I mean, it was physically possible to stay inside at either the old camp or the "new" one. Just like it's physically possible to juggle flaming chainsaws. In both cases, the real question is why you would want to.

SHALL WE GATHER AT THE RIVER?

To give you an idea, picture the housing in *Slumdog Millionaire* as a point of reference. Now, understand that our "new" camp was the kind of place where their poorer relatives in the country would have lived. And *those* folks would have donated their last rupee to someone staying in our old camp. The truth is, both places would have been condemned by a blind Tijuana building inspector.

For one thing, we had long ago handed over the old camp to the wood rats in something of a "land-for-peace" deal. My brother Steve lost the final battle over the bedroom. From there, we retreated onto the porch for a few years and, finally, to a new piece of property altogether.

The new camp offered a couple of advantages, including its convenient location on land we actually own. It was also closer to the water, so the moccasins cut down on the number of rats that lived there full time. Another advantage was that it had walls on only three sides. That made it much more convenient if you had to bolt outside in stark terror when some critter wanted to share your sleeping bag.

I explained to Mary that in our world, the word *camp* was more a geographical reference than an architectural one. And staying inside was a (distant) fourth choice for ways to spend the night down there. A tent was the best option because you could pick it up and shake it out. Once inside, you could zip it up and be

The old camp. *Photo by author.*

21

pretty well assured that nothing was going to come in. (Although that didn't mean rats, 'coons and 'possums wouldn't scratch around the outside all night.)

If you didn't have a tent, the next best choice was to build a big fire and curl up on the ground. A good fire will burn long enough to let you get to sleep. And when the animals do show up, at least you're not trapped inside with them.

Even sleeping in your car is a superior way to spend a night there. Sure, you may be cramped and either sweating or freezing, but depending on the condition of your ride, you can be pretty sure nothing will get in it with you.

In fact, as I thought about it more, I figured out that the only good reasons to stay inside the camp were: You were severely injured there and couldn't move, someone was actively shooting at you and/or you suffered from a crippling case of agoraphobia.

Nevertheless, I'm proud to say that Mary did go, and she was a trouper throughout most of the trip. And I give a lot of credit to my brother Bill for helping her adjust. He was very reassuring, letting her know that there was really nothing in the swamp to worry about. He explained that, despite our kidding, the animals down in the woods were far more scared of us than we are of them. "All except for the flying snakes," he told her. "They can get pretty nasty."

The "new" camp. *Photo by author.*

That was more than twenty years ago. But spending time in the woods remains a strong family tradition. Believe it or not, it's a tradition that Mary now enjoys even more…as she listens to the stories and looks at the pictures I bring home with me.

THE STORY OF POLEHENGE

One feature that Mary and other camp visitors tended to notice immediately was Polehenge, a name derived from a strikingly similar structure in the United Kingdom. Near the English village of Wiltshire are the ruins of Stonehenge, an ancient ritual site featuring giant stone pillars that rise up out of the ground, obviously built by humans but with a purpose that still isn't entirely clear. There are lots of theories, of course. Some claim it was a burial site, while others say it was a pagan temple.

I don't buy any of that. Based on its fraternal twin in Calhoun County, I'm pretty sure it was a hunting camp that never quite got finished. As with

"Polehenge." *Artist rendering by John Paul King.*

its English counterpart, some of the details of the construction of Polehenge have been lost to time. The consensus among the experts—mostly my brothers, family friends and me—is that sometime in the mid-'80s, my father ran into a crew replacing telephone poles along Hugh Creek Road. Somehow, he convinced the foreman to give him several of the used ones and then follow him down to our camp and dig an equal number of holes in a roughly square pattern near the bank of the slough.

Who these people were and how Daddy was able to press them into service remains a mystery. What we do know is that a little while later, my brother Bill and his friend Chuck Reed showed up at the camp and were soon put to work setting the poles in the ground. When they were done, Polehenge was born: nine telephone poles rising from the mud bank (to different heights) and reaching for the sky (at odd angles). It was a sight to behold.

My brother Hentz was so moved that he shared an eerily accurate prophecy: "I guarantee you'll come back here in twenty years, and those poles will still be sitting there just like that." He was right, mainly because Daddy had counted on this being a multi-generation project, one that would culminate with a camp atop the poles he planted. The rest of us just had to build it.

What Daddy failed to take into account, however, is that his sons all remembered long nights with rats and snakes at the old camp. We weren't going to spend time and money just to give them a room with a view (not to mention the high ground if a fight broke out). We were perfectly happy to keep on sleeping in our tents, so Polehenge remained unfinished and mostly untouched until it was finally torn down a few years ago. Sadly, it disappeared having never become a world heritage site, a national park or even a meeting place for drug-addled cult members.

But because of Polehenge, pictures of its forerunner across the Atlantic always leave me wondering what Stonehenge would have looked like if the ancients had ever gotten done with it.

THE BEST SEAT IN THE HOUSE

Another camp oddity was the "throne." I've searched high and low, through stacks and stacks of photos, but I haven't been able to find a picture of it. That's a shame because it was one piece of my father's handiwork that perfectly captured his artistry, ingenuity and attitude. It was a masterpiece of design and functionality that remained a source of entertainment from the time it was built until high water floated it away forever.

The throne was born one Saturday morning back in 1983. I remember because Brad Guilford and I took the day off from bagging groceries at the Piggly Wiggly and went fishing. We had paddled a couple hundred yards from the camp, but we were still close enough that we heard Daddy drive up. As soon as he shut the motor off, we started hearing beating and banging from his direction. There was the growl of the chainsaw, a tree falling, hammering, dragging, more chainsaw and more hammering.

"The Throne." *Artist rendering by John Paul King.*

It was a hot morning, and Brad, being a considerate soul, suggested that we go see if Daddy needed any help with whatever he was doing. "What good could possibly come of that?" I asked. Brad knew my father well and couldn't come up with a good answer. But the heat was getting to me as much as the guilt was getting to him, and eventually we made our way back to the camp.

We were greeted by a sight that's hard to describe with mere words. There before us was Daddy, standing beside an oak stump about two feet tall and maybe eighteen inches in diameter. Nailed to the back was a two-by-twelve that rose a couple of feet above the top of the stump. On both sides were short, upright two-by-fours supporting flat, perpendicular one-by-fours.

Being familiar with Daddy's carpentry and his priorities, I already knew what I was looking at. Brad, on the other hand, was at a loss.

"What in the world is that?" he asked.

Daddy was a bit offended. "Can't you see it's a chair?" As he spoke, he attempted to give his creation a trial run, but he got stopped abruptly in mid-sit. Despite having almost everything else in the world in his truck, the one thing Daddy never carried was a measuring tape. If he had, he would have realized that he didn't leave quite enough space between the two armrests. After some effort, he managed to contort himself into the chair while Brad and I tried not to laugh. (We failed.) Daddy didn't say a word. Instead, he wriggled free from the contraption and gave us a firsthand lesson on how to improvise, adapt and overcome.

He went back to the truck, came back with his chainsaw and cut an arc out of the inside of each armrest. This time, he sat down with no trouble, crossed his legs and pronounced his creation perfectly comfortable. It was a triumphant moment, but for all the years that chair stayed at the camp, that was the last time I ever saw him actually sit in it. Mostly it just served as a fun conversation piece for the rest of its days.

I like to think the throne is now down at the bottom of the slough, with fish swimming all around it. I also imagine them asking one another, "What in the world is that?"

Note: Illustration at the beginning of the chapter "Low Water at the Landing." *Pen and ink drawing by John Paul King (from the original oil painting by Suzanne Conner).*

Part II

THE FISH FRY CULTURE

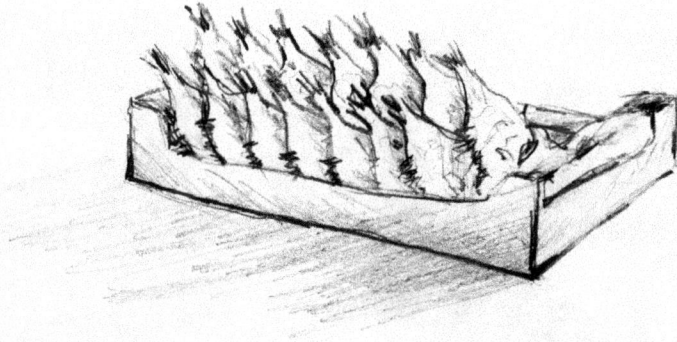

I've never envied the country club lifestyle. Sure, I wish I had country club money, but a country club membership is about the last thing I'd spend it on. Instead, I'd blow it on better guns, bigger boats and longer vacations spent using them. That's because I grew up in a fish fry culture.

At least once a week, my dinner would come from a cardboard beer flat lined with paper towels. On it would be a stack of bream (bluegills), shellcracker (red-eared sunfish) or channel catfish, battered with Hoover's fine ground cornmeal and fried golden brown. There would also be hushpuppies with diced onions and fries that were irregular shapes because they had been sliced with a pocketknife.

Everyone has certain sights, smells and sounds that invoke images of home. For me, nothing brings those memories rushing back like watching a blue propane flame blast a cast-iron Dutch oven full of Sessions peanut oil. I can still close my eyes and see my father sitting in a lawn chair in front of the Iamonia Lake Clubhouse, a gaggle of men telling stories under the old live oak. I can smell the fish as they cook and get faint whiffs of beer and bourbon whiskey wafting on a late spring breeze.

I have only a handful of memories about my grandfather, Daddy Mac, but most of them are of fishing with Mother Mac and him. In fact, some

The fish fry culture is alive and well. *Photo by author.*

of my earliest memories in life are of watching a red cork floating on dark water, waiting for the telltale quiver that signaled a fish bite.

This isn't recreation or a hobby I'm talking about; it's a way of life. Our forefathers had to figure out how to survive on what these swamps and piney woods could provide. Ever since then, catching, cooking and eating fish has been about celebrating nature's abundance and sharing it with friends and family.

The stories in this chapter aim to give you a glimpse inside this culture and what it means to the people here.

WORTH A WHIPPIN'

In the spring of 1943, the fish had started biting, and a group of men in Blountstown were planning an early morning fishing trip and lunch on the banks of the Chipola River. My father was a senior in high school and wanted very much to go with them. The only problem was that the trip was planned for a Friday, when he would be in class.

Andrew Jackson McClellan (center) and family at the Dead Lakes, circa 1915. *Courtesy of McClellan family collection.*

Never one to let education stand in his way, Daddy asked his principal, Jim Ramsey, for permission to skip that day. After all, he would be graduating soon, and it wasn't like he needed to be an A student to fight World War II. Surely one day wouldn't be a big deal.

But education was a big deal for Mr. Jim. He was a big, burly man who was married to one of Daddy's cousins. Mr. Jim had the thankless job of keeping a bunch of rowdy, strapping boys in line so that girls like my mother could actually learn. And although he certainly didn't condone skipping school, he probably figured that having Daddy off campus would be a net positive for the rest of the student body. Whatever the reasons, Mr. Jim eventually decided that my father could have the day off. The only condition was that he would have to bring a note from my grandfather, Daddy Mac, the following Monday. If he failed, it would mean a whipping—which Mr. Jim was more than capable of delivering.

Daddy agreed to the terms, went fishing and had a big time. But late on Sunday evening, he remembered that he needed a note. In a panic, he found Daddy Mac working at his desk and told him about his deal with the principal. Without looking up, Daddy Mac said, "No problem." A few minutes later, he handed my father an envelope addressed to Mr. Jim.

The following morning, Daddy strolled into the school office (with a smug look on his face, no doubt) and handed over the envelope. Mr. Jim opened it up, read it and laughed out loud. Grabbing his oversized paddle, he said, "All right, Gene. Put your hands on the desk."

Shocked, my father said, "Wait a minute! You said if I brought a note, I wouldn't get in trouble."

"Read the note," Mr. Jim replied.

Daddy looked at the slip of paper. All it said was, "Beat hell out of him, Jim."

How Many Fish Make a Mess?

When fishermen in Northwest Florida start talking, inevitably you'll hear the phrase "mess of fish" come up. But just what does that mean?

I went fishing almost every day for a week once, but I never caught what I would consider a "mess" of fish. And with all the fish I wasn't catching, I had time to give the issue some thought. Why didn't I have a mess? At first, it seemed obvious: I didn't catch enough. But that's not entirely true. I probably caught upward of one hundred pinfish. So why doesn't that constitute a "mess"?

I decided that it was because I don't eat pinfish, which means that any valid definition of mess has to include edibility. That makes sense when you consider the military's use of the term—mess hall, mess kit, officers' mess and so on. The problem with this definition is that I did catch some edible fish, just not very many and not very big ones.

At this point, you're probably thinking that, clearly, a "mess" is enough keeper fish to eat. It's a function of quantity and quality. But it's more complicated than that in communities along the Apalachicola River. There, the phrases "enough to eat" and "mess" are used to mean different things. A mess is definitely enough to eat, but "enough to eat" isn't necessarily a mess. Case in point: somebody pulls up to the boat landing, and you ask, "Did you catch a mess of fish?" Often, the answer is, "Nope. We got enough to eat, but that's about it."

So we can assume that a "mess of fish" is *more* than enough to eat. But if that's true, how many more? Is there a definitive number? And what if you have a large family or guests or a tapeworm? Can a mess for one person simply be enough to eat for another? Can two people with enough to eat combine their catch so that one person has a mess?

The confusion doesn't end there, either. There are also qualifiers. For example, you can have a "nice" mess or a "big" mess as well. Again, I'm not

A "mess" of fish. *Photo by Domenick Esgro,* Calhoun-Liberty Journal.

sure where the line is, but I've never heard the word used with a negative modifier. No one I know has ever caught a bad mess of fish (though I have seen folks with a mess of bad fish).

To further cloud the issue, I've noticed that a mess is almost exclusively used to apply to freshwater fish. Does anybody ever say they got a mess of grouper or marlin? On the other hand, I have heard the term applied to speckled trout, so maybe the rule is suspended for inshore fish.

And what about things other than fish? I've killed a mess of squirrels but never a mess of quail—and certainly not a mess of deer or hogs. That suggests that the term also only applies to animals or fish of a certain size.

But then how do you explain a "mess of collard greens"? Now we're in a whole new domain of life. And here again we can have a mess of turnips, but nobody says they picked a mess of oranges or even a mess of lettuce.

Maybe this is one of those enduring mysteries, like why I use live shrimp for bait when I'd rather eat them than most of the fish I use them to catch. I think there is an answer, but it's an elusive one. To paraphrase Justice Potter Stewart's comments about obscenity, maybe we can't really define a mess of fish…but we know one when we see it.

THE PIED BREAM: A FISH OF OUR VERY OWN

For those of us who fish in the Apalachicola River and its tributaries, catching pied or hand-painted bream is one of the highlights of any trip. Some of my earliest and best memories are of holding on to a cane pole for dear life and steering a big pied back to me. That thrill is still is enough to make me drive two hours, bail a boat and fight mosquitoes all day.

It's an experience I enjoy even more knowing that these colorful bluegills aren't found anywhere else. I've heard for years that pied bream are unique to the Apalachicola system, but confirming that information proved to be harder than I thought. So I reached out to the good folks at the Florida Fish & Wildlife Conservation Commission (FWC).

The FWC, as it turns out, was way ahead of me on this issue. Chris Paxton, fisheries administrator for FWC's Northwest Florida region, is very familiar with the pied bream and provided me with a ton of information and the best pictures I've ever seen. (The vivid colors start to fade after the fish leaves the water, so it's hard to get them on camera.)

Hand-painted or "pied" bream versus regular bluegill (left). *Photo by Chris Paxton, Florida Wildlife Conservation Commission, myfwc.com.*

32

Paxton confirmed that you won't find pied bream anywhere outside an area bordered roughly by the Apalachicola River to the east and the Chipola River to the west. He has taken them from the Dead Lakes in the south and Merritt's Mill Pond to the north. He added that they're also found in Ocheesee Pond, but he suspects they were released there.

Interestingly, testing conducted by a University of Alabama researcher in '04 and '05 found that pied bream aren't genetically different from their more ordinary-looking counterparts in the Apalachicola system. So, why do they show the characteristic mottling patterns that make them so unique?

Without getting too science-y, Paxton speculates that it could be a number of factors, from the geology of the river system to diet to sexual dimorphism, changes in coloration related to mating. The latter seems plausible because all the samples he collected were sexually mature males. On the other hand, he said they found sexually mature males without the unique colors as well.

We might never know why pied bream bear their spectacular markings, but what's most important to remember here is that, like tupelo honey, they are another part of our natural heritage that makes the Apalachicola River region so unique in all the world.

BEING PICKY ABOUT PANFISH

I have nothing against crappie, really. They do have the second-worst food name ever, ranking just below *turd*ucken and ahead of *shiit*ake mushrooms, but there's little else about them to not like. For a panfish, they grow pretty big, fight pretty hard and live pretty much everywhere I fish.

That's why you may be surprised when I tell you that a lot of folks who fish the Apalachicola, especially old-timers, won't keep a crappie. Why not? Because in terms of taste, speckled perch, as we call them, just don't match up to bream, shellcracker and channel catfish—their more popular neighbors. For discriminating fish eaters, it's like real Coke versus that cola drink from Walmart.

There are people who travel hundreds of miles and pay lots of money to catch crappie. Bill Dance has devoted at least one full episode of his popular television show to fishing for them. And in every description I've ever read, their table quality is listed as good or excellent.

Even so, old-timers like my grandfather treated them like they might contaminate the rest of his catch if they got too close. And I can remember our father telling me, "Don't put that speckled perch in the basket." In fact, the only acceptable reasons for keeping them were that you caught absolutely nothing else or you were feeding your in-laws that night.

It wasn't just crappie that got thrown back either. Largemouth bass (which my grandmother and others inexplicably called trout) were treated the same way for the same reason. Ditto for warmouth. Keep in mind that these were people who lived through the Depression in the rural South and who would eat most anything that could be loosely defined as food. But they also were people who spent two or three days a week, every week, fishing in the rivers, lakes and sloughs around Calhoun County.

When you do that for several decades, fishing turns into a never-miss proposition. And if you always catch plenty of fish, you can afford to be picky about which ones you eat.

While I agree that bream and shellcracker taste better than crappie, you don't always have enough to be picky. So I occasionally keep the speckled perch, bass and warmouth that I catch. I just try to feed them to someone else.

A Few Things to Understand About Fishing

Being picky about what you keep is just one of the unspoken rules of fishing in the region. There are some other things an outsider might want to know before fishing with a local. I'll use myself as an example, but I'm hardly alone in this mindset. Think of these as explanations in advance for what you can expect.

First of all, terminology is important. For example, you need to know the difference between a good fishing spot and a terrible fishing spot. If we're both catching fish, that's a good spot. If I'm catching fish and you're not, that's still a good spot. You just don't know how to fish. And I don't care if your end of the boat is in three inches of water and under a hornets' nest. We're staying put.

On the other hand, if you're catching more fish than I am, then we are in a terrible spot, and that means we're going to have to move immediately. And don't be surprised if the move consists solely of turning the boat about 180 degrees. You'd be amazed at how fast that can make a terrible spot into a great one.

The author in a great fishing spot. *Photo by Domenick Esgro,* Calhoun-Liberty Journal.

The next thing to understand is our bait situation. Again, it's critical that you know the language. For instance, if I say, "We're low on bait," what that really means is that *you're* low on bait. When I say, "We're out of bait," it means I'm low on bait. When I say, "It's time to leave," that means *I'm* out of bait.

Now, let's go over what we do back at the landing. Say we come back with a mess of fish. Somebody's bound to ask where we caught them. You can say "in the water" or "by a log" or "in the eastern United States." Be imaginative. In fact, there's only one wrong answer, and that's to tell somebody where we actually caught them.

At this point, you may be getting the idea that I only care about myself. But that's not true. You'll see my generous side when we get back on the hill. I'll offer you as many fish as you want. Of course, I'll make that offer exactly once, and it'll be before the fish are cleaned. Afterward, all bets are off.

Finally, let's talk about how the trip is described to others. If we don't catch fish, my story is that I simply went along with you. Even if I kidnapped you at gunpoint and dragged you onto the boat kicking and screaming. If we go and catch fish, then I took you fishing. And it doesn't matter if it was your truck, your boat and your tackle and you dug the worms by hand.

There's an old saying that success has many fathers. But only one can be in the family photo...and that's going to be me.

PUSHING LIMITS AT THE DEAD LAKES

The following story comes with some important caveats: it was told to me a long time ago, it happened a long time before that and the people who were there are no longer with us here.

That said, I have no problem believing this one because it involves my great-uncle, James Fields, a game warden who was known as a stickler for enforcing the law, and my father, who was not known for always following it.

Daddy told me that not long after he returned home from World War II, he went fishing on the Dead Lakes, where there was a limit of twenty-five fish per person per day. But they were biting quickly that day, and it wasn't long before he had twice the limit and still wasn't done. What he didn't

Sunrise on the Dead Lakes. *Photo by Matthew Godwin, Off the Map Expeditions, LLC.*

know was that Uncle James had quietly paddled up and watched him catch enough to know that he was way past twenty-five fish.

Uncle James had always been like a second father to Daddy, but that didn't matter at the moment. He grabbed Daddy's fish basket, counted the catch and dumped every one of them back in the water. To make matters worse, as he wrote out the ticket, he told Daddy, "Untie your boat and head on back to the landing. You're done for the day."

I should point out here that neither of them had an outboard, so going back to the landing meant paddling quite a ways. I guess Daddy was feeling his oats that day because he told me he turned to Uncle James and said, "No, sir. You just threw back all my fish. Now I've got to catch some more."

According to Daddy, Uncle James was livid. "Boy, untie that boat and follow me back to the landing right now!"

Daddy just grinned and said, "If you want me to go back, you can paddle me yourself."

Now Uncle James was fuming. He said, "All right. And when we get back, I'm gonna haul you to jail." He grabbed the line, tied the two boats together and set out for the landing. But Daddy wasn't done yet. As Uncle James paddled in the midday heat, my father propped his feet up, lit a cigarette and opened up a cold beer. Daddy said Uncle James looked back and glared as he saw him relaxed, reclined and smiling in the boat behind him. The farther they went, the madder Uncle James got.

And then Uncle James stopped. "He started figuring how long it was going to take to paddle that far, going that slow," Daddy said. "Also, he got to thinking about how that was going to look when we got back to the hill." I'm sure Uncle James considered just shooting Daddy right then and there, but instead he pulled out his knife.

"Don't you ever let me catch you over the limit again," he said. With those words, he cut the rope and paddled off. Daddy told me he went back to his spot and caught another twenty-five fish—but only twenty-five this time. That's because he knew the most important limit to consider was Uncle James's patience, and he was still way over right about then.

CATFISH BASKETS, TROTLINES AND BUSH HOOKS

Fishing typically conjures up images of rods and reels or cane poles, but in the days before fish farms, the commercial catfish industry was the domain

Traditional catfish slat basket made by Seab Larkins of Liberty County. *Photo by Lisa Golden Bristol.*

of people who fished wooden baskets, trotlines and bush hooks. It was hard work that involved long hours on the water and off.

From an early age, I can remember being fascinated by my Aunt Ann's stories of growing up on the Florida River in southern Liberty County. Her father, Richard Larkins, owned a fish camp there and supplemented his income by catching and selling channel catfish.

For Mr. Larkins, the tool of choice was a cylindrical wooden basket made from thin slats of wood tacked to split vines forming the circular framework. There were two "throats" pointed toward the interior of the trap that the fish could pass through easily going in but that would prevent them from coming back out.

This was and is the only legal catfish trap that can be used on the Apalachicola River and its tributaries. One reason is because the slats allowed game fish, like bream and shellcracker, to escape while keeping the wider-bodied catfish in.

The traps were baited with cheese or cottonseed cakes, and according to Aunt Ann, Mr. Larkins could bring in as much as five hundred pounds of fish in a single day. They would be offloaded from the boat into a wooden fish box at the water's edge. The box, in turn, would be hooked to a truck and towed over logs up the bank. The fish would be cleaned in an assembly line process, boxed up and sent to customers.

Not many people fish baskets these days because of the time and commitment it requires to build, maintain and tend them. Instead, most of us prefer trotlines and bush hooks. A trotline is a long nylon or cotton cord with hooks hanging from lines spaced evenly along its length. It's usually tied off to trees on both ends and weighted in the middle to keep the bait close to the bottom and to allow boats to drive over without snagging it. The bait can be anything from live earthworms or Catawba worms to cheese, chicken livers, stinkbait or soap. Bush hooks are essentially singular versions of the same concept. Find a sturdy but limber branch hanging over the water and drop a weighted line down near the bottom.

As catfish typically feed at night, many fishermen will bait their lines in the evenings and check them again early in the morning. Or if the bite is particularly good, many will check the lines again around midnight to maximize their haul.

For now, most catfish served in restaurants or sold in stores is farm raised. Aquaculture is a big industry, and catfish is a species that can survive in the farm environment. However, catfish connoisseurs will tell you that they don't taste quite the same as their wild-caught kin. That's why I believe we'll see a return to the methods people like Mr. Larkins pioneered so many years ago.

WHY WE HAD TO SHOOT THE FISH

The blackfish left us no choice, really. Bill and I would have been quite happy to let him go on his way. We didn't want him on our trotline any more than he wanted to be on it. Yet there he was and here were we.

What separated us—and joined us—was one hundred feet of thin, white string with baited hooks five or six feet apart. It was a work in progress, interrupted by an early, unwanted arrival—one that had taken the first bait on the line while we were still setting it out.

So here we were in a boat, halfway across a slough, holding the end of a trotline, with a huge blackfish on the other end. To retrace our steps would mean losing the line to unfathomable knots and tangles. But to continue was impossible with the thrashing and shaking on the other end.

We were stymied, confounded and discombobulated. As luck would have it, we were also armed. In the boat was a shotgun and five shells, as it was also hunting season and the wood ducks might drop in before we were through. It had to be done.

Bill tugged the line, and the fish's head emerged for a brief second.

I shot and missed.

Another tug. Another shot. Another miss. And another.

We traded positions.

I tugged.

Bill shot.

The line got steady, and we finished our work.

A few quiet seconds passed until Bill broke the silence. "You know, you just don't see that kinda s**t on TV."

A quarter-century later, we have *Duck Dynasty*.

Newbies.

FISHING FOR SUCKERS

Despite how it may seem to those outside the South, sucker fishing is only about 80 percent as ridiculous as it sounds. There is a real fish called a sucker, and people do catch and eat them. But beyond that, yep, it's pretty ridiculous.

First, some background. Suckers are non-game fish that swim along the bottom of rivers, using their snouts to hoover up everything they can find to eat. In the winter, they travel up small, gravel-bottom streams and lay their eggs among the rocks. Then they swim back into the river like deadbeat parents, leaving their young to fend for themselves. I assume they do this so they don't accidentally eat their own eggs, which, come to think of it, is probably worse than abandoning them.

I have no idea how sucker fishing got its start. I assume, way back when, some smart soul saw all those fish swimming upstream and said to himself, "Self, there's only one way those fish can get back to the river." And with that, I envision him standing there for days, waiting for them to swim back by so he could grab them with his bare hands. At some point, I'm sure a much smarter person came up with the idea of using a piece of chicken wire to stop them from getting into the river and another to keep them from going back upstream.

Traditionally, when the suckers were running, a group of men (because women were usually too smart for this sort of thing) would gather at the creek bank, build a fire and net or gig the fish. If necessary, young boys could be sent into the ice-cold water to fetch them up by hand (because boys were dumb and readily available). The fish would be cooked and eaten on the spot but only after cleaning and "gashing" them. In addition to being ugly, suckers are also bony. So much so that the best way to cook them is to leave the bones in and make diagonal cuts through them. Deep fried, the fish can then be eaten bones and all.

As a teenager, sucker fishing didn't hold much fascination for me. That time of year, I was thoroughly focused on hunting and have the grades to prove it. On the other hand, it was something to do in Blountstown on a Saturday night in winter. So occasionally Gary Wayne Purvis, Brad Guilford and I would go after them the hard way—by wandering around Fox and Wildcat Creeks with flashlights, trying to gig them. This, of course, always ended with us coming home late, soaking wet and fish-less. (Because why wouldn't you push one another into freezing water in the middle of the woods at midnight?)

One night, however, GW and I set out to do it up right. We camped out on the Chipola River and set up a monofilament version of chicken wire across the creek. A novice might have mistaken this for a gill net, but I can assure you, based on a discussion with my lawyer, that it was chicken wire… with a lead line along the bottom and a cork line across the top. In fact, it remains the most effective chicken wire I've ever caught fish in to this day.

That night, we got at least a dozen big suckers, but there were only two of us and we didn't bring anything to cook fish with. Plus we had to go out that night because there was a remote possibility of meeting girls.

The next day, we hunted for a while, packed our stuff and went home with a cooler full of uncleaned suckers. GW had generously decided I should take them, in part because he had done a big sucker cookout the weekend before but mostly because I think he knew what was going to happen next.

When I got home, I brought the ice chest to the door to show my father. "What should I do with them?" I asked (with no small amount of pride in my voice).

Daddy looked in the cooler at the day-old fish and said, "You can go dump 'em right back there in the woods."

"What?" I couldn't believe it.

That's when Daddy explained that suckers are only "okay" under the best circumstances—right out of the water and straight into the grease. They go from edible to much less so with every minute that passes after that. He said the real reason people ate suckers is because by midwinter, the good fish like bream aren't usually biting and that was about the best option available. Although he didn't mention it, I suspect that it also was a good excuse to hang out by a fire on a cold night, drink liquor and laugh at your offspring splashing around in freezing-cold water while trying to catch fish with their bare hands.

As I look back on it, fishing for suckers is a pretty good description of the whole exercise. The trick is not to be the sucker.

THE MARVELOUS MULLET

Mullet are the Rodney Dangerfield of the fish world. They just don't get any respect, or at least not as much as I think they're due.

Seriously, when was the last time you heard Roland Martin or Bill Dance say, "Today, we're going after the elusive, hard-fighting black mullet"? Have you ever seen one mounted on somebody's wall? Does anybody every charter a mullet boat? Of course not, and that's a shame because while other fish are getting all the attention, the lowly mullet has been quietly feeding our families for years.

Mullet are unpretentious, workmanlike fish. If they were people, they'd be the kind of folks you'd want as neighbors. The quiet kind who keep their yard mowed and don't complain when your dogs dig up their flowerbed. Or sue when your son's band practice causes them permanent hearing damage.

Mullet on a cleaning bench. *Photo by author.*

Mullet are plentiful, travel in bunches and even jump out of the water to let you know where they are. They're good to eat smoked or fried. And they can live anywhere, from the saltiest ocean to the freshest springs.

As a result, mullet have always been the fish of choice for anyone who has to feed a large crowd. In fact, I'm not sure it's possible to run for office in Northwest Florida without holding at least one mullet fish fry.

Mullet don't ask a lot in return either. You don't need an expensive boat and high-dollar fishing tackle to bring home a mess. A cast net or a snatch hook will do just fine. And although I've never done it, I'm told mullet will also bite a hook if you use the right bait.

But how do we humans show our appreciation? Several years ago, the State of Florida tried to get folks to start calling them "lisa" because it didn't think "mullet" sounded appetizing. (According to Lisa Bristol, who told me that story, all it really did was irritate a generation of young women who happened to share the name.) To add insult to injury, mullet also became the pet name for one of the most embarrassing hairstyles in history. (Second only to the tonsure or "monk cut"—bald in the middle, fringe on the sides.)

I've never understood why mullet are regarded so poorly, while marlin, tarpon and bonefish are virtually worshiped—and nobody even eats them.

Well, except for the guy in *The Old Man and the Sea*, and Hemingway was probably drunk when he wrote that part.

In traveling to all corners of Florida during my career, I've decided that I could probably live anywhere that mullet are considered good food. When I walk into a restaurant and see mullet on the menu, I know I'm around my kind of people.

On the other hand, if it's a seafood restaurant that doesn't serve mullet, I know to double-check my bill. People who don't respect mullet are the kind of people who charge you extra for hushpuppies and make you sweeten your own tea. And we all know that's just wrong.

JIM HENTZ: FISHING AT ONE HUNDRED

I don't know what anyone else plans to be doing when they're one hundred, but I expect to be fishing. Now, before you laugh, let me explain that there is historical precedent here. My Uncle Jim Hentz, for whom I was named, continued to hook up his boat trailer and drive to his favorite fishing holes until shortly before his death at one hundred years old.

At his funeral, the preacher told the story of Uncle Jim showing up on his doorstep bright and early one morning the previous summer. Thinking he was there for a visit, the preacher invited him in. It turned out that Uncle Jim's trailer had jumped off the hitch near the preacher's house. He just needed some help hooking it back up so he could get on with his fishing trip.

Uncle Jim was my mother's older brother, and he lived for a century even though he was born in 1906, when just surviving childhood was an iffy proposition. "Old school" doesn't begin to describe him; he was more like Old Testament. His faith, hard work and determination enabled him to establish a successful grocery business during the Depression. Later, it would grow to multiple stores and shopping centers in the Panama City area. He was even shot during a robbery once, but it didn't slow him down or change the way he conducted his business. When he retired from the grocery business at age eighty, he immediately turned his attention to real estate and did just as well at that.

The one thing Uncle Jim wasn't was a talker. He was unfailingly polite, sharp as a tack and stayed up to date on politics and news. But he didn't believe in idle chatter.

One night when I was in college, my mother called and said that Uncle Jim wanted to speak with me. In years past, that always meant one thing: he was planning a fishing trip to Iamonia Lake and wanted me to bail out and clean up the old boat he kept there. But that didn't make sense because I knew he had bought a brand-new one. When I called him later, our phone conversation went like this.

"Uncle Jim, Mama said you needed to speak to me…"

He said, "I got a new boat. Do you want the old one?"

"Yes, sir. That would be great."

"Well, come down here and get the motor and title, too."

I started to thank him profusely. "Uncle Jim, I really appreciate this and I'll…" and then, *click*. Silence. Our business was done, and he had better things to do than listen to his nephew babble on.

A few years later, my brother Bill and I caught a mess of fish down at the camp using crickets. We paddled up to the landing just as Uncle Jim had finished launching his boat. We shook hands and exchanged pleasantries when I noticed that he had earthworms for bait.

I asked him if he wanted the twenty or thirty crickets we had left, and he replied simply, "Nope. Don't want to give 'em a choice." That was in the early '90s, but it was only later that I figured out that what Uncle Jim meant was he didn't want to give himself the choice. He had made a decision to fish with earthworms, and that's just what he intended to do, whether the fish liked it or not.

Later that same day, I got another reminder of the kind of man he was when I tried to help him out of his boat. I extended my arm just in case he needed the support. He ignored my gesture, jumped out of the boat and shot me a look that is burned into my memory to this day. Without saying a single word, he let me know that was as close to a whipping as I had come in a long time.

Of course, that was back in his younger days. When he was only eighty-six.

Note: Illustration at the beginning of the chapter "Fried Bream on a Beer Flat." *Artist rendering by John Paul King.*

Part III

HAVE GUN, WILL EAT

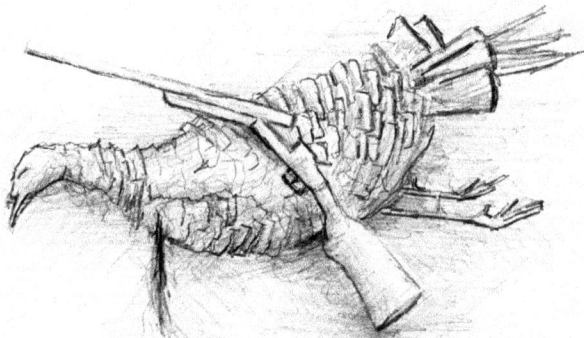

If you had to walk into the river swamp and walk back out with a meal, the evidence suggests that a cane pole might be your best weapon of choice. The old-timers figured that out long ago, which is why most of them eventually fished more than they hunted.

Think about it. Let's say you've got three hours or so in the morning or evening. If the fish are biting at all, a person who knows what he's doing can fill a fish basket with bream and shellcracker, clean them and feed his family a delicious meal before the sun goes down.

Hunting, on the other hand, is a less certain, more time-consuming activity. You might stay in the woods all day and never see a deer or turkey. Or the wind might pick up and make it hard to even kill a mess of squirrels.

Still, hunting has always been important in the Apalachicola River Valley for the food it provides and the rituals associated with it. Turkeys, bears, deer, squirrels, rabbits, doves, quail, ducks and even raccoons and 'possums have been part of the diet here since time immemorial. (Although the deer population was nearly decimated in the early part of the twentieth century, and turkeys were threatened as well. Bears have made a comeback, but there has been no open season in Florida since 1994.)

In the days before food plots and tree stands, most hunters were opportunists, like the Native Americans who came before them. Back before

Calhoun County educator and historian George Atkins (left) and Jack Atkins with turkeys. *Courtesy of Chris Atkins.*

World War II, the typical hunter in Northwest Florida carried a shotgun with birdshot for small game and buckshot for larger animals. He might carry a turkey wing bone to use as a call if the opportunity arose, but for the most part, what he hunted was what he saw.

Of course, in the days of smaller truck farms and fence rows, there were organized dove hunts, and many folks owned bird dogs to even the odds on quail. But the most important part of that equation was that people produce food to show for their efforts.

This chapter is a tribute to the generations who taught us how to take our guns to the woods and come back with dinner—or at least a really good story about why you didn't.

DEER HUNTING THE WAY IT WAS

I consider myself too young to be nostalgic about very many things. As far as I'm concerned, every typewriter ever made can rust in the dump or rot in hell, and I won't miss them at all. The same goes for eight-track players, pet rocks and mood rings. On the other hand, the art of hunting and killing deer—or "harvesting"

Florida deer hunting as it once was. *Photo by Charles Barron, courtesy of State Archives of Florida, Florida Memory, http://floridamemory.com/items /show/75013.*

them (for the politically correct)—has seen some changes that I don't consider improvements. Some things were better back in the day. For example:

There were fewer deer. Thirty years ago, deer hadn't reached nuisance levels yet, and killing one required much more patience and time in the woods. It just doesn't seem right nowadays for eight-year-olds to have trophy racks hanging on the wall. Deer used to be a game animal that you worked your way up to after killing and cleaning squirrels, rabbits, hogs and maybe a few doves, ducks and quail thrown in. It took time to get good enough to kill a deer, mainly because…

Hunting meant exactly that. Many years ago, only farmers or landed gentry hunted over food plots. In fact, only a handful of people in my hometown had enough land, time or money to actually plant food specifically for deer. Most folks hunted by either running dogs or, as we did, slowly slipping through the woods at daylight and in the evenings hoping to see a buck. Which is why…

We shot any buck with visible horns. And by "visible" I mean just enough showing to tell your family and friends with a straight face that you knew it was a buck before you shot. Of course, bucks were one thing, but…

Shooting a doe was a cardinal sin. Okay, so maybe this part isn't better, per se. Still, staring at dozens of does and yearlings over the course of the season was an exercise in frustration that built patience. Don't believe me? Ask any old-school hunter about "growing horns" on a deer. Trust me, it happens. But it just made shooting a buck even more satisfying. So…

We were proud of little spikes and four-points. We cut the horns off every one of those deer and tacked them on the wall like they were bull elk. Eternal life and enduring fame for a young buck could be had just by standing in my crosshairs. And that was okay because…

It wasn't all about the antlers. Seriously, it was about the total experience, the tradition of self-reliance and the appreciation for what it once took to put meat on the table. Sure, we all wanted to kill the biggest buck, but if anybody ribbed you about the size of your deer, some old-timer would say, "That's all right, boy. You don't eat the horns." However…

We ate the deer—and everything else we killed or caught. To men of my father's generation and older, that was the point. It was R&R to be sure, but for the most part, they considered a trip to the woods a mission. It was successful if you came back with something to eat. And that meant…

We weren't ever exclusively hunting for deer. Easing through the woods meant you might see hogs or turkeys, or you might just decide to shoot a mess of squirrels. The point is that, even if the deer weren't moving, you still didn't have to come home empty-handed. But if you did, there was always tomorrow or next weekend because…

We hunted close to home. Very few people traveled to Texas or Nebraska or other deer meccas. As a result, our only points of comparison were the deer killed by other folks hunting in the same places we did. Yes, we had *Outdoor Life* and *Field & Stream*, but in real life, we stood as good a chance of dating a *Playboy* model as killing one of those giant bucks. After all…

We didn't know anything about Quality Deer Management. If someone ever said they passed up a big buck because his antlers didn't have enough mass—or because his inside spread wasn't big enough—we would have figured he was lying and left it at that.

Deer are wild animals, not livestock. Despite all the science that has gone into improving their genetics and growing the herd, I hope the "wild" part never changes.

THE DEER THAT GOT AWAY (AND THE SQUIRREL THAT DIDN'T)

My three oldest brothers—Mack, Hentz and Steve—spent a lot of time hunting with our father in his younger years when he was still as enthusiastic about hunting as he was fishing. The flipside is that, according to them, he wasn't nearly as patient back then. As evidence, Mack and Hentz have both told me about the first deer they didn't kill together.

As young teens, our father took them to the camp to go hunting. The plan was to drop off Mack on one of the old roads going down to the slough. Daddy and Hentz then rode farther up the swamp, where he was going to put Hentz out.

As Hentz tells it, after Mack got out, they had only gone a few hundred yards when Daddy hit the brakes, pointed out the window and said, "There's a buck right there. Shoot him." Hentz pointed his shotgun out the window in that general direction, but all he could see was trees. "Shoot him!" Daddy said, now with even more enthusiasm. Hentz still didn't see the deer. "Boy, he's right there. Shoot him before he runs off."

At this point, Hentz decided his best move would be to just fire off a shot into the trees. When he did, the buck magically appeared, nowhere near where he'd aimed and now on a dead run through the woods. He shot a couple more times just for good measure. When it was obvious that the deer was still in excellent health, Daddy let fly with his favorite expression: "My achin' back."

Then it occurred to him that the deer was headed directly toward where they had put Mack out just a few minutes before. "Maybe Mack will see him," Daddy said. As soon as he said the words, they heard a shotgun blast from that direction. "Ha! I bet Mack got him," Daddy said. And with his hope for the next generation restored, they drove back as fast as they could.

Sure enough, there was Mack, standing in the road with a big grin on his face. According to Mack, he could see Daddy smiling, too, as they rolled up. But the smile suddenly disappeared—right when Mack held up the fox squirrel he'd just killed.

According to both Mack and Hentz, the ride home was pretty tense that day.

You Can't Hide Luck

In the thirty-six years we shared on this planet, I can only remember two items of camouflage clothing that my father ever owned. There was an old pair of pants with a World War II–era pattern and another pair I bought him years later as a Christmas present. He would wear them now and then, but he never believed camouflage clothes were a hunting necessity.

On a normal workday, you'd find Daddy dressed in khaki pants, a colored short-sleeve shirt and Hushpuppies, the official shoe of old men. His hunting ensemble was just older versions of the same items, along with a brown jacket and the latest baseball cap someone had given him.

Daddy came up during the Depression, when not everybody in Calhoun County even owned a pair of shoes, much less special clothes for hunting. He learned to kill squirrels, rabbits, quail, doves, ducks and turkeys wearing whatever he had on. As a result, he felt like camo was more of a fashion statement than a real advantage in the woods. His usual comment on the issue was, "If you'll learn to be still, look and listen, it won't matter what you wear." What he conveniently left out was the disclaimer, "As long as you're as lucky as I am."

People who hunted or fished with Daddy regularly soon learned that incredible, inexplicable good luck followed him most everywhere he went. He liked to tell a story that happened at Horace Travis's camp, an old wooden structure on stilts toward the south end of Iamonia Lake. Each year, Daddy and his friends would stay down there for about three or four days at the beginning of hunting season. There would be a big barbecue on Friday night for anyone who wanted to come. Saturday lunch would be a giant pot of squirrel and rice.

Daddy followed his father's footsteps into this gathering and, like him, became the "head chef." That meant he had to spend a lot more time at the camp than anyone else, but it didn't mean he couldn't hunt.

One cold morning, most of the group had come back from hunting and gathered by the fire. Someone looked up and pointed out a buck deer standing in the woods not seventy-five yards away. Everyone scrambled to find their guns, except for Daddy. His old Winchester Model 12 was leaning on the tree next to him. He calmly picked it up and killed the buck without leaving his chair.

Daddy liked to tell that story to emphasize the importance of being prepared, but to me it just drove home the point that he led a charmed life. I got undeniable proof of that during a dog hunting trip back when I was in college.

McClellan Swamp is a big swath of land between the Apalachicola River and Hugh Creek Road, just south of Blountstown. Our cousin Pete McClellan had owned the property and still had hunting rights. He had a group of friends that included Steve Marchant, Joe Wood Sr., Henry James Chason, Reddin Brunson, Gary and GW Purvis and a few others who hunted with deer dogs on the property. As was so often the case, Daddy also served as the camp cook for this bunch and would occasionally take me with him.

I've never been much of a dog hunter, but I always enjoyed hearing them chasing the deer, barking up a storm and changing directions. All the hunters would be spread on roads and trails across the property, hoping that the deer was a buck and that the dogs would run it past them.

One morning, Steve, the group's nominal leader, decided that he didn't have enough people to properly cover the block of land where they were going to release the dogs. Meanwhile, Daddy was setting up his cook station that included his gas cooker, ice chest, lawn chair, folding table and small television set that he hooked up with cables to his truck battery. He was planning on cooking and watching football and didn't have much interest in leaving.

But Steve was adamant that he needed another person, so Daddy grumbled and agreed to go. I rode with him about a quarter mile down an old two-trail road. He stopped and said, "Get out here, and I'll drive on up the road a ways. If the deer comes by, just make sure he's a buck before you shoot."

With that, he drove away, and I found a comfortable spot by a log and listened for the dogs. Naturally, they had turned and were heading well away from Daddy and me, so mostly I just sat still, watching and listening, enjoying the sounds of nature.

Nature soon got interrupted with about four or five successive rifle shots coming from Daddy's position up the road. I knew the dogs were going the other way, so at best I thought he might have shot a couple of squirrels. The worst-case scenario was that he had just dropped the hammer on a bunch of hogs I would have to clean later. After a few minutes, I heard him blow the horn. Expecting the worst, I walked down the road to where he was.

I can remember that scene as vividly as if it were yesterday: The truck is parked facing me. The door is open with the television on the front seat, facing out. Daddy is sitting on a log, watching a ballgame, with a cigar in one hand and a Natural Light in the other. He's wearing a pair of light-blue pants, gray-brown Hushpuppies, his jacket and a ball cap. His old, beat-up .22 Magnum is propped on the log next to him.

When I got to the truck, he said, "I want you to start at this log and walk that way," as he pointed out into the woods. "Go until I tell you to stop and count your steps."

I had no idea where this was going, but I did as I was told. When I got to fifty steps, I turned and looked back at Daddy. He waved and said, "Just keep walking." I got to seventy-five steps: "Keep going." When I got to one hundred paces, I started to worry because his eyesight wasn't that good. Nevertheless, he said to keep going.

When I was about 120 yards away, he said, "Whoa! Now look around right there." To my utter shock and disbelief, there at my feet lay a six-point buck, dead as a hammer, with four bullet holes in and behind his front shoulder. I dragged him back to the truck, and Daddy told me that he had seen him slipping through the woods from a pretty good ways off. When he realized that the deer wasn't going to get any closer, he picked out a clearing ahead of the buck and waited. With iron sights on a .22 magnum, Daddy shot him as soon as he came out into the open.

It was some impressive shooting, and Daddy was determined to milk it for all it was worth. When we got back to the camp, he drove right up into the middle of the crowd, got out of the truck, pointed to the back and said, "Here's your damn deer. Now, y'all don't interrupt my game again."

We had a good laugh as Steve put into words what everyone else was thinking. He threw his hat on the ground and said, "That's it! I'm gonna get rid of all these dogs, burn my camo and come rolling down here about 8 instead of 4. I'm gonna get me some light-blue dress pants and Hushpuppies just like Gene's, sit on my butt and watch football."

I remember thinking, "Yep. And if you're as lucky as he is, you'll still kill deer."

TELLING THE TRUTH ABOUT THE TURKEY

As noted earlier, my Aunt Ann grew up in a fish camp on the Florida River in southern Liberty County. Her father, Richard Larkins, had carved a homestead out of what is now the Apalachicola National Forest, near the small community of Sumatra. As the crow flies, Larkins' Fish Camp was about twenty miles northwest of the legendary Tate's Hell swamp in Franklin County. It is a remote enclave even today.

As Mr. Larkins's only two children, Aunt Ann and her sister, Maretta, had to pitch in and help run the family businesses: the fish camp, a restaurant and a commercial catfishing operation. Mr. Larkins also had a herd of hogs that had to be tended to. They bore his registered earmarks and roamed free in the swamp most of the time. But when the river was high, the hogs would get stranded. That meant the girls would have to miss school to help round them up and move them to high ground.

Growing up in that environment, Aunt Ann learned how to handle a boat, shoot a gun and build a wooden fish basket if the game warden might find it (or a wire basket if he wasn't around). She also knew how to clean fish, hogs, deer and every other animal that might be found in the woods or the water. Fortunately, the list included turkeys. That came in handy when I killed my first one at age fifteen and desperately needed a reliable co-conspirator.

The problem started one afternoon during hunting season when I walked up on a group of about ten or eleven turkeys feeding in a dry creek bed. Without even thinking about it, I shot the turkey closest to me. I was incredibly happy…for a brief moment. And then two facts reared their ugly heads. First, my turkey was a hen, which had long been illegal to kill. But that was secondary to the bigger issue: Florida didn't even have a fall turkey season in those days. This was during the period when the state was working desperately to restore its populations, and I had just taken a beautiful young female right out of the gene pool.

Desperate, I hid the turkey in my jacket and slinked back to my friend's truck. All we had to do now was get home. But getting stopped en route was only a remote possibility. My father becoming howling mad, however, was not. So, I had to figure out what to do with the still-warm game law violation in my possession.

There was only one person I knew who had the skills, sympathy and good judgment to help me out: Aunt Ann. So rather than going home, I went straight over to her house, where she patiently listened to my sad story and said, "The first thing let's do is clean the turkey."

And clean it we did. Aunt Ann didn't believe in just taking the breast meat, like some folks do today. She boiled water to scald it and had me pluck it. Then we singed it. Then we pulled any remaining pinfeathers with needle-nose pliers. After I pulled the guts out and washed it up, it looked as good as any of its kin at the meat market.

"Now, take it back to your house and put it in your daddy's outside freezer," she said. "Just wait until he's in a good mood and then tell him what you did, that you're sorry about it and that you know better than to do it again."

I went forth armed with her advice but nervous nonetheless. Prepared for the worst, I told Daddy that I had killed the turkey, but he cut me off before I could say any more.

"What did you do with it?" he asked.

"It's in the freezer. Aunt Ann helped me clean it." That was all he needed to hear.

"That's great! We'll cook him on Christmas morning." Not only was I off the hook, I had apparently scored some major points as well. Although, he did say, "Now, don't go telling everybody you shot a turkey and don't shoot any more."

After I told my brothers this story, they explained to me what I think Aunt Ann suspected all along: Daddy cared a lot more about the quality of the meat in the freezer than the path it took to get there.

CULTURE CLASH: THE BLOODY BRONCO BREAKDOWN

If you ever want to feel completely stripped of your manhood, you can either start carrying a toy poodle around in a handbag or get a minivan. I never tried out the poodle idea, but I can vouch for effects of the minivan.

By 1996, Mary and I had three small kids, and fate forced me to give up my four-wheel-drive. I replaced it with a Ford Windstar, which was like having the word *domesticated* tattooed across my forehead. To be honest, Mary drove the van most of the time, but that just meant I had to drive our little red Toyota, which was almost as bad. It was a compact four-door car that got great gas mileage and ran well. It was incredibly practical, but it still looked like something a teenage girl would drive.

Obviously, I needed a change. So, I traded the Toyota for a late '80s model full-size Ford Bronco that was jacked up to accommodate extra-large mud-grip tires. The carpet was gone, the seats were ripped and there was mold growing in several places. Nearly everything inside was electric, and almost none of it worked. Plus, it had an exhaust leak that made it sound like a machine gun when you revved the engine. In short, it was perfect.

Not surprisingly, Mary didn't share my fondness for the Bronco. I even explained that it had a bench seat in the front, so she could sit right next to me. All she said was, "Good. I'm sure your next wife will enjoy that. I'm not riding in it." And she stuck to her guns for most of the time I had it.

One Monday morning, however, I had to go out of town for business. It would have been cheaper to charter a jet than buy that much gas for the Bronco, so Mary decided she could handle driving the old blue beast for one day and let me take the van.

I should pause here and add a couple of important details. First, I had gone hunting in Blountstown the day before my Monday trip. I killed a deer, field dressed him and, with no one around to help, dragged him up onto the tailgate of the Bronco and into the back. The second thing you should know is that the back window of the Bronco opened and closed electronically—but only when it felt like it. And it didn't feel like it on the way back from Blountstown.

The next day, when Mary left to drop the kids off at preschool, she tried closing it to keep from smelling the exhaust. At first it didn't work, but just as they got to the car line, she finally got the window to roll up. Big mistake. Remember the deer? Well, apparently a lot of its blood seeped into the tailgate of the Bronco. When Mary hit the switch, the window emerged from its slot, covered in all the grossness left behind from the deer.

She said it looked like something out of a horror movie. I can only imagine the looks on the faces of the uptight, yuppie parents at the school. The Bronco might as well have had "Helter Skelter" painted down the side. Right about then, Mary was mad as a hornet, and I was in Jacksonville, happily unaware.

As soon as the kids were dropped off, she went straight to the nearest car wash, slammed the door and in an angry growl said, "I need this truck washed really good, right now. And make sure you get every bit of that blood off." Mary said the guy slowly backed away and asked if she was all right.

She thought he was acting a bit odd, but he got right to work cleaning the old vehicle.

It didn't dawn on her until a few minutes later that he probably figured she had just killed someone and dumped the body. He obviously didn't want to be the next one to take a ride in back.

Much to his relief, Mary finally explained about the deer. She also promised him that if there was ever going to be a dead person in the back of that vehicle, it would most certainly be the guy who made the mess, not the one cleaning it up.

SEASONS CHANGE, PEOPLE DON'T

Here in Northwest Florida, we haven't forgotten the true significance of Thanksgiving. Even as we gorge ourselves on fried turkey, barbecue and assorted veggie-and-cheese casseroles, we always remember that the last Thursday in November also marks the first day of general gun season in Zone D. We can look forward to four days of hunting—interrupted only by food and football—followed by a two-week hiatus before it starts up again in December.

Because I'm sentimental about history, I want to point out to younger readers that it hasn't always been this way. There was a time when the season started on the first or second weekend of November and ran until early January. Most of us who hunt regularly were happy about that change because it extended the season into February, when the deer up here start the rut.

The only person I know who had any trouble with it was my father. In early December several years ago, a friend of his named George Burch flagged him down as Daddy was driving down Hugh Creek Road. George was opening a smokehouse, and he had a special offer: If Daddy killed a deer, George would clean it, grind it up and make smoked venison sausage, all for fifty-five dollars.

The "cleaning" part was all Daddy needed to hear. He was already on his way to the camp and had a doe tag in his glove compartment. He wasn't even gone an hour before he came driving back up to George's place with a big doe in the back of his old Bronco. I saw George a couple of weeks later, and he recounted the conversation when my father drove up.

Daddy: "Here you go, George. I got a doe in back."

The creek behind the camp in winter. *Photo by Maria Rogers Heil.*

George: "Gene, that's illegal."

Daddy: "No it's not. I've got a doe permit right here."

George: "That's fine, but it isn't hunting season now."

Daddy: "What?"

George: "Gene, hunting season ends after Thanksgiving weekend. It doesn't come back in until the middle of December."

Daddy: "When did that start?"

George: "About five years ago."

Daddy: "Well, they didn't tell me. Now, come get this deer. I want to get home before the football game starts."

I don't ever remember him saying it, but Daddy probably should have been thankful that Calhoun County didn't have more game wardens. I'm pretty sure George was thankful, at least right then.

I Don't Know Ferrell and I Didn't Shoot His Pig

I was reading one of the many articles about the problems caused by "feral pigs," and I started trying to remember when that phrase came into general usage. It certainly wasn't when I was a kid. Back then, we hunted "wild hogs," and they fell in place right behind deer and turkeys on the Most Important Game Animals (MIGA) scale that I just made up. Hogs enjoyed an honored status above squirrels, rabbits, ducks, doves and quail, so killing one was a big deal in my world. That's why it seems disrespectful now to put them in the same category as runaway house cats.

I never use "feral pigs" to describe wild hogs. But as I think about it, there are other pig-related terms we do use here that might be confusing to folks who don't hunt hogs or those who read *Field & Stream* and such. Here's something of a glossary of words you'll hear from those of us who hunt in the Apalachicola River swamp.

Feral pigs feeding. *Photo by Lane Stephens.*

BOAR/BOAR HOG: Others use the term "boar" or "wild boar" to refer to any wild hog. Granted, it sounds more menacing than feral pig, but I use it to mean a male hog of any age. I don't usually shoot boar hogs because their meat tends to be gamey and tough. But if you want a mean, nasty-looking mount for your fight club, pool hall or sports bar, a boar hog will fill the bill nicely.

SOW (pronounced like *south* without the *th*): You may hear this term used to describe any female hog. When I say it, it refers only to a female that has or has had pigs. Growing up, most folks wouldn't shoot them because they may have a litter or be pregnant. (Believe it or not, back then we wanted to make sure there were enough of them.) Boar hogs look menacing, but sows with pigs can actually be more aggressive.

PIGS/PIGLETS: A hog is a full-grown pig. As in the example above, we use pig most often to mean piglet.

GILT: If you're hunting hogs to eat, this is the one you want. It's a young adult female hog that hasn't had pigs yet. Here's a good way to tell: Look at her teats. If they are elongated, she's probably a sow. If not, she's likely a gilt.

SHOAT: A shoat is an adolescent hog, older than a pig but not full-grown. When we talk about shoats, we're usually referring to a hog that isn't big enough to shoot. (Meaning that the amount of meat isn't worth the trouble to clean.)

BARROW: This is one you don't see much of in the wild anymore. When I was younger, though, a lot of folks would trap hogs, castrate the young males and release them. Like oxen, this allowed them to grow large and fat rather than muscular and tough.

It bothers me that hogs have become such a problem lately, especially since banning hog hunting is one of the ideas I've seen for controlling their population. One dubious theory is that hog hunters are trapping and releasing feral pigs on private property as an excuse to hunt them. That may well have happened, but I doubt it accounts for the dramatic increase in the hog population.

A more likely explanation is that not enough people still appreciate the experience of hunting them. And maybe that's because we started calling them feral pigs.

NEVER TRUST A SQUIRREL

I'll be the first to admit that I've built up a lot of bad squirrel karma over the last forty years or so. In fact, if the Good Lord is a lover of limb rats, I'm going to need a lawyer with me at the Pearly Gates. On the other hand, if squirrels do go to heaven, I can claim credit for a lot of them getting there a little sooner than planned. In my defense, however, I think more people ought to know that squirrels are evil little critters themselves, and I have a bunch of experiences to back up that statement.

Let's start with the fact that they are unrepentant vandals. In my last house, they were able to outsmart my ace Labrador retriever (not a difficult task) by running back and forth along the top of the fence. When Pete got too tired or bored to chase anymore, they would sneak across the yard, climb the chimney and gnaw their way into my attic. I only discovered this because they also chewed an escape route through the ceiling on the back porch.

In case you're wondering, a squirrel infestation doesn't improve your property values. I have no idea what made my attic so appealing. For all I know, they could have been running a meth lab up there, but they might just as easily have been plotting to murder me in my sleep. Based on what I've seen in the woods through the years, I'm certain it's the latter.

Folks who hunt the varmints will back me up on this statement: squirrels know when you're hunting them versus larger game. Take a .22 and slip through the woods, and they disappear faster than my paycheck. Go deer hunting with a high-powered rifle, though, and you'll be overrun with bushy tails, bouncing and barking in the branches above you.

But that's not all they're doing. They are also actively plotting your demise. I learned that years ago as I sat under a white oak tree hoping a big buck would wander by. The deer didn't show up, but a battalion of squirrels came out and, for a little while, provided some high-quality entertainment. The first thing I saw was two chasing each other from tree to tree. One made a long leap to a thin branch, with another in hot pursuit. That's when I learned that squirrels might be great climbers, but even they miscalculate occasionally.

Squirrel Two jumped for the same limb as Squirrel One. Squirrel One made it (barely), but when he landed, the thin branch dipped way down under his weight. By this time, Squirrel Two was already airborne, expecting the limb to be where it was when he took off. It wasn't.

Squirrel Two went skydiving without a parachute for about ten feet and hit the ground with a *thud*. To his credit, he scurried right back up the tree no worse for the wear. While all this was going on, I didn't notice that three more of their buddies were hard at work about fifty feet up in the tree above me.

At first it seemed innocent. An acorn dropped a few feet to the right of me. Nothing unusual. Then another fell on my left. Another hit on my right, this one a little closer. One dropped on my left, closer still. When the next one hit me on the leg, I suddenly realized they weren't being clumsy—they were actually dialing in their shots like an artillery spotter. I looked up just in time to see one dragging a limb as big as he was, fully intending to crack me over the head with it. I started to shoot him on principle, but even back then, .243 ammo was twelve dollars a box; I figured it would be easier to just move.

Ever since that day, though, I've approached squirrel hunting with an entirely different attitude. It might be a sport to some folks, but I figure it's a matter of civil defense—stopping them before they develop heavier weapons and better aim.

Surely the Almighty makes allowances for that.

LIFE LESSONS FROM THE WOODS (AND WHAT I LEARNED INSTEAD)

Nature is a wonderful teacher, but she isn't certified in special ed. Challenging the notion that anyone can learn, here's a sample of some of the woods wisdom that was wasted on me.

The Lesson: You might think Catawba worms are gross, but fish love them.
Should have taught me: *Being successful means paying attention to what others need—your spouse, your friends, your customers and so on.*
What I actually learned: If you don't poke the hook all the way through, less green goop gets on your hands.

The Lesson: Squirrels may be the only animals on earth with a shorter attention span than a ten-year-old kid.
Should have taught me: *A little patience pays off when you're hunting.*
What I actually learned: Shooting a .410 into a treetop will make squirrels move so you can see them.

The Lesson: Despite their name, oak snakes will climb most any tree.
Should have taught me: *Never trust labels or make assumptions based on them.*
What I actually learned: Oak snakes have sharp teeth and strong jaws.

The Lesson: A tiny twig poking you will eventually feel like a large knife stabbing you.
Should have taught me: *Little problems turn into big problems if you ignore them.*
What I actually learned: They make hunting vests with seat pads now!

Nature's lessons are best learned with boots on the ground. *Photo by Ella McClellan.*

The Lesson: Owls don't make any noise when they fly, but they do when they eat.
Should have taught me: *Some people tell you what they're going to do; others show you what they've done.*
What I actually learned: Never trust an owl.

The Lesson: Enough mosquitoes swarming around you can drown out every other sound.
Should have taught me: *Your biggest problems are sometimes just an accumulation of little ones.*
What I actually learned: A Thermacell is thirty dollars well spent.

The Lesson: If you believe the fish will bite, you'll keep your line in the water longer.
Should have taught me: *Just believing in success can give you the patience to keep trying until you actually succeed.*
What I actually learned: Fishing in the same spot despite not catching anything is a sign of insanity.

Fortunately for me, nature does offer unlimited remedial courses, so I intend to keep studying as much as possible.

How to Lose Your Mind in a Duck Blind

A professional trainer warned me once that my yellow Lab, Pete, might not have the stuff great dogs are made of. In the years since, I've witnessed him nearly drown trying to retrieve a bait bucket tied to a dock and swim halfway across Santa Rosa Sound because he thought I was throwing the mullet that were jumping.

Now that he's older, I've made peace with the fact that Pete is basically a sentient throw rug. But in his first two years, I still had hope that he was going to be a great hunter. After three months of work and a small fortune spent with the trainer, I was assured that Pete was fully "started." All he needed was some actual hunting experience to polish his skills.

Somehow I took that to mean I should take Pete on a real hunt where I expected to shoot ducks and have him retrieve them. Turns out that was a huge mistake. What the trainer should have said instead was, "If you work with Pete constantly over the next several years, it's possible he won't be a complete liability in the field." Sadly, I didn't realize that before his first hunt.

Thus, with great enthusiasm, I went out to the pond the day before the season opened, set up my blind in a prime spot and even put an auger in the ground to which I could attach Pete's leash. I knew that young dogs often "break" and go fetch before they are given the command. What I didn't know was that breaking early would be the least of my problems.

Well before daylight the next day, our party assembled at the barn, and we let the dogs run off some of their excess energy. For about half an hour, Pete and the other two dogs ran around in circles getting warmed up for the intense action ahead.

Duck blind on a beautiful morning. *Photo by author.*

In retrospect, I should have let Pete run for about three or four hours. Instead, we went to the blind and hunkered down to wait for the ducks. For the first twenty minutes or so, everything was going as planned. Pete sat beside me quietly, leashed to his auger and behaving like he was generally happy with the whole state of affairs. I couldn't have been more proud—I was in my blind with my genuine duck dog, waiting for first light. It was a peaceful, perfect *Field & Stream* moment. Right up until the first birds came in.

Just before dawn yielded to day, a flight of wood ducks came whistling in at low altitude directly above us. Pete started whimpering nervously and tugging at his leash. Since legal shooting time was still a few minutes away, no one fired, and the ducks landed safely. But Pete was on edge.

When a second wave of woodies came screaming in, the guns erupted and so did Pete. It's not that he was gun shy. He just wanted in on the action. And forget "breaking" a little early—Pete wanted to literally snatch the ducks out of the sky.

He began barking and whimpering uncontrollably. (For any non-hunters reading this, that's not generally considered helpful behavior on a duck hunt.) At this point, he was trying his best to leap out of the blind. I couldn't shoot because I had to use one hand to hold his collar to keep him from actually pulling the auger out of the ground.

It got worse from there. Several more flights of various types of ducks were coming in well within range. But I was trapped in the blind with ninety-five pounds of hyper-excited dog attached to one hand and a shotgun in the other. I felt like a pro bull rider with his arm caught in the ropes.

The combination of my left hand, his leash and the auger were just enough to control Pete's front end, but his hind legs and tail were a different matter. With all his thrashing about, he was able to jump-kick in a full circle and totally destroy my blind during the struggle. I had no choice now but to put my gun down and use both arms and my body weight to subdue him. Meanwhile, some of the ducks were flying close enough for me to feel the water coming off their wings.

Picture this, if you will: It's dawn on a small farm pond, with eight or nine hunters carefully hidden around the edges. Ducks are coming in like it's the Atlanta airport, and the gunshots make it sound like the Fourth of July. On the west side, exposed to God and all the world, is a guy losing a spirited wrestling match with a big yellow dog. A dog, by the way, that sounds like he's being neutered without anesthesia.

I really didn't want to screw up everyone else's hunt—or, worse and more likely, get shot by "accident"—so I did the only thing I could. I grabbed Pete's leash and hustled him off a couple hundred yards out in the woods, where he continued to howl and bark like he had been kidnapped. He and I sat underneath the pines for the next two hours, listening to what turned out to be a fantastic duck hunt—for everyone else.

I would like to tell you that I spent that time reassuring Pete that he was a good dog and that I understood his youthful enthusiasm. In truth, I sat there considering how long it would take me to drive to North Georgia and drop him back off with his trainer. I even went so far as to compose a threatening note in my mind. I can't remember all of it, but I do remember the gist: "Give me my money back or I'm leaving this dog with you."

Later, I took Pete on an easy, two-mile walk. When we got back home, he plopped down on the cool tile of the kitchen floor, exhausted from his "workout." I petted him, watered him and gave him a snack while he lay there. I also wiped my feet on him just for good measure. He wagged his tail as if to say, "See, I'm useful!"

WILDLIFE HERO JAMES R. FIELDS

Although I never knew him, I owe a lifetime's worth of thanks to my great-uncle, James Fields. That's because Uncle James was the man who instilled in my father a passion for hunting—a passion that he then passed along to my brothers and me. Whether that was a blessing or a curse is up for debate, but there's no doubt that he has had a profound influence on three generations of my family.

From an early age, my father would spend weekends during hunting season with Uncle James and my Aunt Alyese. As soon as he was old enough to make the trip by himself, he would come home from school on Friday, grab a bite to eat and walk the eight miles or so from Blountstown to their small, cinder block house south of Hugh Creek. My grandmother told me she usually wouldn't see him again until well after dark on Sunday.

In exchange for helping Aunt Alyese with chores, Uncle James would loan my father a shotgun and give him exactly ten shells. But the rule was that he had to account for every shot he took. Either bring home an animal or bird or an unfired round. A miss would mean one less shell the next time out.

Daddy told me about that rule one day as we were driving past a large live oak tree in a field near Uncle James's house. "If I shot and missed while I was hunting, I'd stop by that tree on the way home and wait for doves to land," he said. "I'd let them get close enough together so I could kill two with one shot. I didn't want to bring home an empty shell with nothing to show for it."

Eventually, my father graduated, left for service during World War II and returned home to marry my mother in 1946. That same year, Uncle James got hired as a game warden with the old Florida Game and Freshwater Fish Commission. The state needed skilled woodsmen with unquestionable integrity—men who were smarter and tougher than the outlaws who roamed the river swamp back then.

According to most folks who knew him, Uncle James was overqualified by all those standards—especially the integrity part. In fact, he threatened several times to arrest my father, his own protégé and nephew. One such occasion was an evening when my parents had Uncle James and Aunt Alyese over for dinner. My mother said Uncle James was very complimentary of the dozen or so wood ducks she'd cooked, and he suddenly became more interested in them after my father left the room.

"Those ducks sure were good, Betty," he said. "Lots of them, too. Did Gene kill 'em all?"

My mother, possibly the worst criminal accomplice in history, said, "Oh, yes. He got them all yesterday."

"All of them?" Uncle James asked. "By himself?"

My father overheard enough of the conversation to figure out what was going on. He came bursting back into the room in time to explain (or invent) his side of the story: he'd been hunting with several of his buddies, who had—in an uncharacteristic moment of generosity—decided to give him all their ducks.

"If he hadn't already eaten some of the evidence, Uncle James probably would have called around to see if I was telling the truth," Daddy said. "He didn't put up with anybody breaking the law, especially not his kinfolks."

In the end, his passion and commitment to justice would cost Uncle James his life. On Christmas Eve 1950, he became only the fourth Florida wildlife officer to be killed in the line of duty—shot to death at night, pursuing a poacher through what is now the Apalachicola National Forest. He left behind a wife and three young children. I can only imagine the nightmares they must have relived every Christmas for years to come.

It's human nature to try and make sense out of a tragedy like that or to draw a broader lesson from it. Obviously, it speaks to the danger that comes with being a wildlife officer and to the courage of the men and women who do that job every day.

But in my opinion, it wasn't Uncle James's death from which we should learn the most. Instead, it was his life and the lessons he passed along to my father, and thus to my brothers and me, that are most valuable: Don't waste a shot. Don't waste an animal. Be accountable. And carry out your duty with courage and integrity.

All of us should strive for a legacy like that, no matter how long or short our time on earth turns out to be.

WILDLIFE ANGEL BETSY KNIGHT

I've always believed that the world could do with fewer activists and more people of action. That's especially true when it comes to wildlife. Plenty of folks are willing to protest against wearing fur, hunting animals, eating meat or whatever the latest trendy issue happens to be. But there are precious few willing to devote their lives to actually helping ill, injured and orphaned animals.

Betsy Knight was one such person, and her passing in February 2012 was a great loss for her human friends and family, as well as for the extended family of wild creatures she helped and healed over the past forty years. Betsy was the executive director of the Big Bend Wildlife Sanctuary and one of Florida's most active rescue professionals.

Just to be clear, I'm not talking about nursing the occasional baby bunny or squirrel back to health. Betsy rehabilitated and released animals like black bears, white-tailed deer and various birds of prey—critters that were quite capable of maiming or killing her. And at seventy-three years old, she was doing that well

Wildlife rescue legend Betsy Knight with Florida black bear cubs. *Courtesy of Betsy Knight family.*

past the age when most folks would have called it quits.

People who care about bears should also know that Betsy's work shaped Florida's official policy for handling orphaned cubs. Before her, a lot of folks thought that bear cubs raised by humans couldn't be released into the wild. It was Betsy Knight who proved they could.

I knew Betsy as an eccentric cousin, family friend and local legend. She was proud of her work and would talk about it with anyone who asked, but it was clear that she wasn't in it for fame or fortune. Betsy's passion was helping animals, plain and simple. In her field, she was outspoken but not obnoxious. She was self-confident but not self-righteous. Most important, she didn't demand respect; she earned it with hard work, every day.

And here's a twist: Betsy was also a hunter. Some might see that as a contradiction, but to her it was common sense. She knew that humans must be both protector and predator. She also understood that hunters play a vital part in managing wildlife populations and funding conservation efforts.

To Betsy, hunters and wildlife share a common enemy in unrestricted development and habitat destruction—actions she fought as an educator and advocate. Her grace, charm and sharp wit made her a natural in that role.

I often think about Betsy when I see some teary-eyed celebrity asking for money or some B-list starlet posing nude for PETA. Their gestures are shallow at best and self-serving at worst. By contrast, Betsy's legacy is her deeds, not her words. That's why her work will live on long after Hollywood's attention shifts to the next shiny object.

As much as I'll miss Betsy, I take comfort knowing that if angels really have wings, she's probably mended a few already. And if animals get to go to heaven, they've got a friend waiting when they get there.

Note: Illustration at the beginning of the chapter "Old Tom and a Long Tom." *Artist rendering by John Paul King.*

Part IV

WHAT THE GOOD LORD PROVIDES

Aman named E.E. Callaway once wrote a book that speculated that the biblical Garden of Eden was located in Liberty County near the current location of Torreya State Park. In his book, Callaway laid out an impressive list of reasons, including the presence of the Florida torreya tree, which he claimed was the gopherwood tree mentioned in the Bible. There was also the physical description of the lands near Eden that seemed to match, as well as the presence of rare plants that lent more credence to his claims.

Callaway's theory has its supporters and its skeptics, but I'm among the many who believe it doesn't matter. The area is close enough to Eden for our tastes. It's a land of abundance for those who know where to look and what to look for and, more importantly, those who find joy in the simple act of looking.

These are stories about the bounty of the land and how it takes unexpected forms and requires unusual methods to obtain—how it's sometimes there for the taking and sometimes comes to us.

Tupelo Honey: A Season with the Bees

Imagine going to work knowing that someone was going to sneak in and slap the ever-lovin' snot out of you thirty to forty times a day, every day. There's nothing you can do about it, and you don't know when or where it's going to happen—just that it will, a lot.

If that sounds appealing, beekeeping may be your dream job. Except that instead of hard slaps, it's painful stings that interrupt your day. There's no retaliation because the bee dies shortly afterward anyway. For you, it's a few minutes of burning pain. For him, it's a kamikaze attack. I know this because at thirteen years old, I spent a tupelo season working for Charlie Cook Bridges, a Chevron distributor in Blountstown and my father's long-suffering best friend.

As I remember, the interview and selection process went something like this: Daddy came home one spring afternoon and said, "Charlie Cook's coming by in a little while to pick you up. You're going to work in the bees with him." I took some time (about a second) to consider all my options (none) before delivering my carefully worded counteroffer ("Yes, sir").

I'm still not sure if Charlie Cook considered my service partial repayment for all the hardship Daddy put him through—or if I was just one more on his long list of McClellan-related burdens. Whatever the case, I've never had a better boss, teacher or workmate than Charlie Cook. You'd also be hard-pressed to find anybody more entertaining. However, by my first night on the job, I realized that my relationship with the bees wasn't going to be nearly as pleasant. That part became clear when we moved them.

Since tupelo season lasts for only a few days to a few weeks, the bees had to be moved to wherever the trees were blooming. But the only time all the bees are in the hive is at night, so that's when we had to do it.

The problem is that bees really don't like being disturbed any time, especially after dark. They make that pretty clear by crawling out of the boxes and blindly stinging anything that isn't another bee. It may not sound like an efficient strategy, but I can vouch for its effectiveness. My beekeeper's uniform helped protect me somewhat. However, with several thousand bees attacking, a few dozen were bound to get through.

Moving the bees often lasted until the wee hours. Once they were in the right place, we had to get the titi, gallberry and other less-desirable honey harvested so that the bees would fill the hives with tupelo. To do this, we placed boxes with empty frames on the hives and took the full ones (minus bees) back to the "honey house," a concrete block structure where

Matthew Godwin of Off the Map Expeditions holds a tupelo branch. *Photo by author.*

we worked in ninety- to one-hundred-degree heat. Charlie Cook used a hot knife to unseal the combs, and I ran the stainless steel centrifuge that extracted honey from the frames. We also collected the excess beeswax, which is used in everything from makeup to candles and soaps. Pound for pound, it was worth as much as the honey, so we took care not to waste it.

Working in the honey house was easier than moving bees, but it had its own set of challenges. For one, it was too hot to wear protective clothing, despite the large swarm of bees that loitered there. Adding to the misery was a thin layer of honey that coated everything in the place, including me.

On a normal evening, I'd usually get stung first by a bee under my collar, inside my shirt or in my hair. My reaction would be to dig the stinger out with my honey-covered hands. The honey, in turn, attracted yet more bees, and so on. Also, it seemed that anything I grabbed invariably had a bee attached to it, making my hands frequent targets as well.

This went on every day of the week, but I got used to the grind and even the stings. Soon, the reddish "bakery grade" honey began to take on a lighter color; before long, pure, golden tupelo began flowing by the barrelful. This is the same honey that years later was the subject of the movie *Ulee's Gold*, and eating it since childhood has spoiled me forever. As far as I'm concerned, there is no better honey in the world.

That's why I'm happy now to see tupelo honey and the people who produce it getting the attention and respect they deserve. It's a unique natural treasure, produced by hard work, fraught with financial risk and physical pain.

I'm also very proud to have worked with Charlie Cook Bridges in his last tupelo season. That experience taught me a lot, including how to suffer through a little pain and how to keep working until the work is done. Those skills have helped me in every job I've had since.

Working in the bees convinced me of something else as well: If I were a beekeeper, Bill Gates wouldn't be able to afford the honey I produced.

FROG-GIGGING BASICS

Pretty early in my professional career, I realized that the subject of frog-gigging wasn't a universally accepted topic of conversation. In fact, as soon as the words rolled off my tongue, I felt like I was speaking a foreign language. The more I tried to explain myself, the worse it got. "You mean you spear the frog?" "Eww!" "You eat the legs?" "Gross."

At that point in my life, I felt like a pariah because I had unintentionally revealed that I wasn't a product of suburbia like my colleagues. Now I realize that I had been given an incredible gift that they would never understand or appreciate. Money could buy me the things they had, but nothing would give them the experiences I enjoyed growing up. And one such experience was gigging frogs.

Frog legs just happened to be my father's favorite food ever, so he had a vested interest in teaching my brothers and me how to find, kill and clean them. The concept is pretty simple: get a boat, a light and a gig. When it's good and dark, ease along the banks of a pond, lake or river. Shine the light until you see their eyes. Move close enough to see the whole body and spear the frog. Lather, rinse, repeat.

Do this accurately about twenty-five to thirty times, and you've got enough frog legs to feed a large family. However, just because the concept is simple doesn't mean it's always easy. For one thing, humans aren't the bullfrogs' only predator. In fact, they're like the French fries of the swamp. Just about everything that eats anything also eats frogs. Included in that list are gators and snakes (winners of nature's "Least Likely to Cuddle" prize). So it pays to watch where you put your feet and hands. And even

Fat bullfrog taken off the creek bank. *Photo by Domenick Esgro,* Calhoun-Liberty Journal.

though it can be hot at night in a Florida swamp, I don't recommend jumping in the water to cool off.

Frogs eat bugs, so it should come as no surprise that some of the best nights for gigging are the times when mayflies and other insects are swarming... and you're holding a light. Just make peace with the fact that you will swallow a bug or two.

Another issue is that spearing a frog with a gig can be harder than you think. You want a long gig pole so that you can get to the frogs in hard-to-reach spots. But what you gain in reach, you lose in steadiness. That's especially true on a small boat with a couple of people in it. Just be careful because if you swing the front end of the gig hard to the left or right, the back end is going to sweep across everyone behind you in the darkness, often stopping upside your partner's head. Make peace with profanity as well.

With regard to the light, headlamps are okay, and even an ordinary flashlight will work, but with a spotlight you will find more frogs, and you won't have to guess whether that's a water snake or a cottonmouth on the branch you're drifting toward.

A good light will also help you see the frogs when they're facing away from you. The white belly stands out against the bank. But let him turn

You have to get down and dirty sometimes to come home with frogs. *Photo by Domenick Esgro,* Calhoun-Liberty Journal.

even a few degrees, and suddenly he looks a lot like everything else on the bank. Frogs that learn that trick can live to be a ripe old age.

Even after you've speared the frog, things can still go wrong. You might think he's dead, but he's really just waiting for you to take him off the gig. If you aren't careful doing that, he'll jump right back in the water. And it's generally considered poor form to gig the same frog twice. They're also pretty quick learners, so getting a second shot is rare.

Cleaning the frog is pretty straightforward, but it's a pick-your-poison proposition. You just need a sharp knife to cut the legs off, and some folks like to do this immediately. The advantage is that you know the frog won't get away. The disadvantage is that it makes a mess in the boat. Once you've done that, however, you can use your fingers or catfish skinners to pull the skin down over the legs. (It's like pants-ing a leprechaun.) Some folks will snip the feet off first, but purists eat them too.

The frog has one last act before he's done: his legs might move a little once they're in the hot frying pan. Don't worry, though; at this point, he probably won't jump out and run off.

Lots of people eat frog legs, but for the overwhelming majority of them, the story begins with tender, golden-fried hunks of white meat, plated well and served with a crisp white wine. I've come to realize that there are only a

Frog-gigging isn't for people who keep their boats spotless. *Photo by author.*

select few who have made the journey into the swamp and taken the frog on his home turf. It used to be a source of embarrassment that I'm one of them. Now, however, it's a source of pride.

How to Stalk and Catch the Elusive Wild Scallop

Like frogs, scallops are one of those culinary treats in our region that are either there or not. There's no real trick to getting them other than dodging stingrays and other scallopers. Nevertheless, I feel the need to share some of my forty-plus years of scalloping experience with a series of questions and answers about the "sport" of scalloping. Consider this a public service to the novice scallop hunters out there. Let's get started:

- Are these really questions you've been asked about scallops? *No, not really.*
- Did you instead invent a series of silly questions that no sane person would ask? *Yep. Pretty much.*
- Is scallop hunting dangerous? *Yes. In fact, scallops are America's fourth-deadliest bivalve, behind only oysters, clams and mussels.*
- Are there any other American bivalves? *Not that I know of.*
- Has anyone ever been injured by a scallop? *Yes. A friend of mine suffered a nasty head wound from a scallop attack.*
- Did the scallop really attack? *Actually, no. Another friend threw it, but the incident was still listed in the official record of mollusk-related injuries.*
- Is there really such a record? *No, not really.*
- Where's the best place to go scalloping? *The best place is any reputable seafood store. A very distant second option is to snorkel in the grass beds from the canal at Mexico Beach in Bay County to the southern border of Hernando County.*
- Is Hernando really a county in Florida? *Apparently so.*
- Can you scallop in other areas of Florida? *Sure. You may be arrested, thrown in jail and fined though. So you should probably stick to the aforementioned area.*
- What is the minimum amount of equipment necessary to take scallops? *One working hand and arm and a dive flag. Masks, snorkels, fins and a bag are nice-to-have accessories. And a boat also opens up a lot more options for scalloping locations.*
- Are scallops hard to catch? *Yes, scallops are the only bivalves that can actually swim.*
- What is the daily bag limit on scallops? *Two gallons of scallops in the shell per person. One pint of cleaned scallops per person. There is also a boat limit of ten gallons of scallops in the shell.*
- Is that a "mess" of scallops? *No. The official term is a "s**tload."*

- How long does it take to gather that many scallops? *It varies but normally about the same amount of time it takes to get a third-degree sunburn on your back.*
- How long does it take to clean ten gallons of scallops? *Depending on the number of people involved, anywhere between twelve and twenty-four beers.*
- How many scallops in the shell does it take to get a pint of scallop meat? *A s**tload.*
- How many calories are in each scallop? *Trick question. Science has proven that simply thinking about scallops burns more calories than you gain by eating them. Thus, scallops can technically be considered a weight-loss treatment.*
- What "science" has proven that? *Shut up.*
- Bay scallops are very small. How do I get the half dollar–sized scallops like they serve in restaurants? *Go to a restaurant.*
- How do the restaurants get them? *Using stingrays and a cookie cutter that's about the size of a half dollar.*
- Did you do any actual research before writing this? *Yes.*
- Did that "research" involve more than one Google search for scallops? *No, not really.*

COLLECTING CATFISH "PEARLS"

Catfish produce pearls. Seriously. Shiny, hard, teardrop-shaped pieces of calcium that range from the size of a grapefruit seed to the size of a marble, based on the ones I've seen.

I came by this knowledge while fishing with my brother Steve one evening in Santa Rosa Sound. After catching a pretty large saltwater catfish, he told me that these otherwise undesirable fish had pearls in their heads and asked if I had ever seen them. I was skeptical, and with good reason. He and my other brothers had me convinced as a child that "Later Claus" was coming the day after Christmas to take back all my toys. I don't take the bait as easily these days.

But Steve cleaned the catfish and then started digging around near where its spine ends. Sure enough, within minutes, he produced two shiny orbs that were as hard as oyster shells and looked and felt for all the world like pearls.

As soon as I got home, I started searching the Internet for more information, but there was hardly any available. I did find an old *New York Times* article from about 1910 or so that discussed catfish pearls being the next big thing.

Apparently the *Times* was wrong because after that, I found nothing about a burgeoning catfish pearl market.

So, one night I went on my own pearl-diving mission inside a freshly caught catfish. It took some effort, but eventually I produced the pearls. The best way to get to them is, well, to dig around the inside of the fish's head about halfway between the eye and the dorsal fin at either side of the spine. Keep digging until you find them. Since then, I've learned that the "pearls" are actually called otoliths and are part of what amounts to the catfish's "inner ear." If you've never handled a catfish before, be careful because the fins are mildly poisonous. (If you have handled a catfish before, you know that "mildly" means it still stings like hell.)

The pearls are pretty, but I don't see them becoming a hot commodity any time soon.

BOUNTY FROM THE BAITWOODS

For as long as I can remember, folks in Calhoun and Liberty Counties have bragged about having the best earthworms in the world. I'm not sure how that was determined, but it's a mark of distinction, and having used other worms from other places, I'm now convinced it's true.

Most of the worms we get come from the Apalachicola National Forest, where lots of people still earn their livings by grunting for worms in the rich, wet soil. The town of Sopchoppy, over in Wakulla County, even has an annual Worm Gruntin' Festival to celebrate the invertebrates.

This might seem silly to some, but as I've traveled the state and beyond, I realized that whether it's true or not, a lot of people visit Blountstown specifically to buy earthworms. But what makes them different from other worms?

"They're tougher, stay on the hook better and stay alive in the water longer," was the answer I got from Bob Smith of Pensacola, an avid bream fisherman who often stops in Calhoun County on his way to Lake Panasoffkee in Central Florida.

Wigglers, the earthworm's squirmier cousins, also make good bait, and a lot of folks keep worm beds specifically to grow them. But they're smaller, and it's harder to get them on the hook and make them stay there. By contrast, earthworms are long and fat and seem much more willing to do their jobs. But earthworms don't come free. That's because gathering them isn't as simple as raking the dirt around.

Earthworms straight from the baitwoods. *Photo by Patricia Swain/Brenda Hill, State Archives of Florida, Florida Memory, http://floridamemory.com/items/show123672.*

Grunting worms is usually done by driving a stake deep in the ground and rubbing it with a piece of metal or wood to create vibrations deep in the soil. As the ground shakes, the worms come to the surface, where they can be picked up.

When I was growing up, going to the baitwoods—as we called the national forest—was an honest, reliable source of income for many. There were a few professionals who had taken it on as their life's work, but there were also folks who were between jobs and needed cash. The earthworm business didn't require anything other than the will to work hard. It was our version of day labor, supplying a product for which there was an incredible demand. It was also another example of how the land itself provided for the needs of its people.

CARING ABOUT CATAWBA WORMS

Earthworms, wigglers and crickets were the baits of choice for most people in the Apalachicola River Valley. But another popular bait was the lowly Catawba worm.

It had been years since I fished with or even thought about Catawbas. Then a friend of mine returned from a fishing trip and showed me some pictures of really nice bream and shellcracker he caught. I asked about bait, figuring he used crickets, but to my surprise he talked about "these yellow and black caterpillars" that were crawling all over some of the trees on the property. "They were called guitar-ber worms or something like that," he said.

"You mean 'Catawba' worms," I said.

"Cwa-tar-ba worms?"

"No, Catawba," I said, carefully pronouncing each syllable. "I think it's really supposed to be Catalpa, but over time both pronunciations have become commonly accepted."

"Wait," he said, "is it Catalba or Catawpa?" At that point, I gave up. "Whatever they are, the bream and shellcracker seemed to love them," he said. The conversation reminded me that when I was very young, I hated fishing with Catawba worms.

Crickets were just bugs, earthworms reminded me of spaghetti and wigglers were squirmy balls of fun. But every time I put Catawba worms on the hook, I felt like they took it personally. For starters, they held on for dear life to the cage or the branch with whatever they use for feet. Crickets and wigglers are always trying to escape, but the Catawbas' only defense was to get a tighter grip. Well, that and producing their Martian-green goo. I was never sure if that was blood or guts or what, but I didn't like it. And I especially didn't like turning them inside out.

Fortunately, by the time I was about ten, I had gotten over my squeamishness and used them whenever I had a chance. But the truth is that I didn't pay too much attention to them even then. They were just good fish bait that we'd go snag off special trees every once in a while. Soon after that conversation, I ran into another friend at Iamonia Lake. He had a few Catawba worms but said they were getting harder to come by lately. The two discussions led me to do some research on the subject.

What I found was some information from a man named Stephen Peele (www.mushroomsfmrc.com) in Pensacola. Mr. Peele has done quite a bit of firsthand research and has actually written a book about the worm. He's concerned that the Catawba/Catalpa is becoming endangered.

According to Peele, the Catalpa worm (actually a caterpillar) turns into a Catalpa or sphinx moth, which feeds in the evenings and lays eggs in the trees. The eggs hatch, and the young caterpillars feed on the leaves of the tree until they're old enough to crawl down into the ground, where they

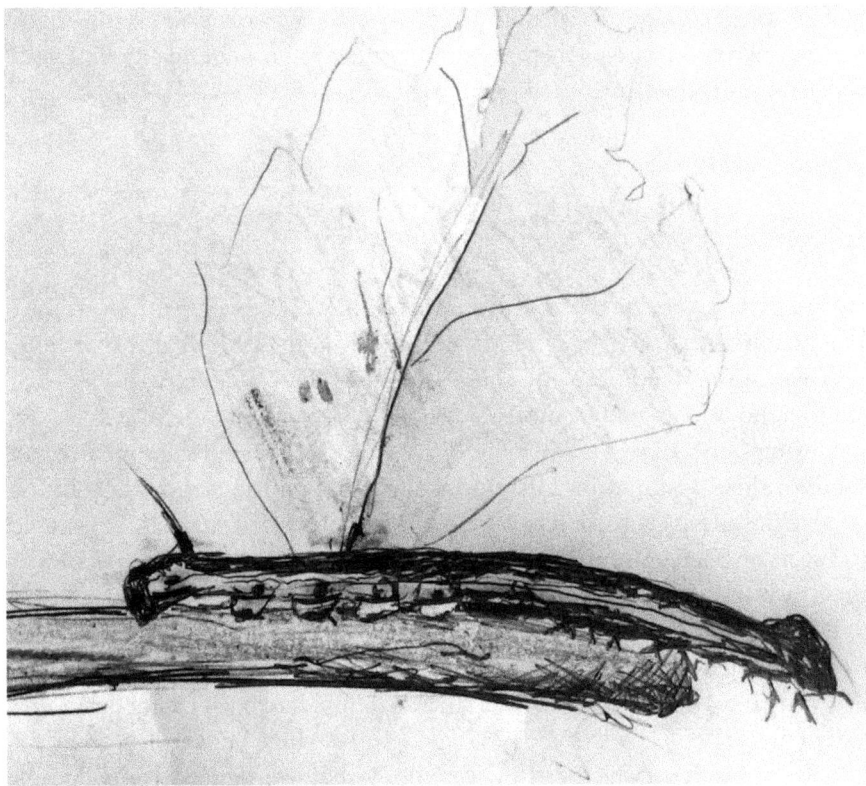

"Catawba on a Branch." *Artist rendering by John Paul King.*

enter their chrysalis phase. Later, they emerge as moths, and the process starts again. He has found no tree other than the Catalpa that will serve as a host for them.

Peele points to insecticides, especially mosquito spraying, as one potential problem for the critters, while predators are another. Birds, beetles and ants, he says, can also wipe out entire colonies and interrupt the process.

Another problem for this favorite fish bait is ignorance. Some people mistakenly believe that the Catawba worms are killing the tree by eating the leaves. In fact, I read one story about a woman deliberately spraying her trees to get rid of them. She learned better, but at the expense of thousands of worms.

Peele is working to reestablish his own Catalpa crop, poisoned by the power company, but he says that it takes a decade to get a productive tree from seed. Planting cuttings can shave some time off that process, but it takes some effort—effort that fewer and fewer people understand or are willing to undertake.

The message I got from this is that if you have a supply of trees and worms, take good care of them. No matter how you pronounce it, those little yellow-and-black Catawbas are gold on the end of a hook.

THE BIGGER THE BAIT...

It's hard to overstate the entertainment value of growing up with Gary Wayne Purvis as one of your best friends and running buddies. For one thing, GW was spring-loaded to go fishing anytime, night or day, year-round. For another, he usually had a good idea where folks were catching fish and how.

During our senior year of high school, for example, he suggested we set some trotlines at Iamonia Lake to take advantage of a steady drop in the Apalachicola River. Folks had been tearing up the catfish, and we wanted to get in on the action. It's just that there were a couple of things standing in our way.

Issue one was that the people catching the most fish were using crawfish for bait. Issue two is that everybody in town knew about issue one. Thus, every ditch between Wewahitchka and Marianna had been cleaned out, and we spent the better part of a day dragging up a whole bunch of nothing.

So, we headed back into town to buy what we figured were inferior earthworms, pretty sure we were going to miss out on the big-time fish

WHAT THE GOOD LORD PROVIDES

catching. Author's Note #1: At that point, neither of us had ever had any issues with using earthworms before.

As we were cruising down Hugh Creek Road, though, Gary Wayne slowed down and said, "You know who's got a bunch of crawfish—Joe Wood." It was true. Mr. Joe was an early adopter and started crawfish farming long before Cajun cuisine even came to Blountstown.

We stopped by Mr. Joe's house, told him what we wanted to do and asked if we could buy some crawfish. He just chuckled and said, "Boys, y'all can have all you want. Just go out there and get 'em out of the traps. But I suspect they're gonna be too big to fish with." We thought he was kidding (as he was prone to do). In our minds, there was no such thing as a crawfish that was too big. Author's Note #2: At that point, neither of us had actually seen a farm-raised crawfish before.

So, we paddled out to the first trap, and as I started to pull it up, I thought we had hit the mother lode. Based on the large, writhing mass, I figured there must be about one hundred in there. There were actually five. Five really big crawfish. I'm talking one dress size smaller than a Maine lobster. There was a brief debate on whether it was even safe to let them in the boat with us. But we'd come too far to turn back now. We checked a couple more traps, wrestled about a dozen more into the cooler, thanked Mr. Joe and headed off to set our lines.

They were so big that we gave some serious thought to shooting them before putting them on the hook. But Gary Wayne nixed that idea because "we might come back and find one with a channel cat in each claw." That didn't happen, but we did manage to catch the world's largest speckled perch on one of our lines. He was at least four or five pounds, and we were pretty proud until we got back to the Clubhouse and showed off our catch.

Author's Note #3: At that point, neither of us had ever caught a striped bass on a trotline before.

WHEN LIFE HANDS YOU A RABBIT

In terms of animal decisions, it may have been the worst case of bad timing since unicorns missed the Ark.

Picture an ordinary rabbit making his evening rounds, chewing on some greenery at the edge of a clearing and watching out for hawks and owls and such. Now let's suppose this clearing is actually a trailer park, and the

85

greenery is my brother's lawn. If you're in any suspense at all about how this story ends, then you didn't know Bill back around 1977 or so.

At that time, he and his wife were newlyweds struggling to make ends meet. (Although Bill probably wouldn't admit they were "struggling" then. I think he describes that period more as "scratching a broke ass with both hands.")

Times were hard in general, and this particular month they had to choose between gas and groceries. As a result, the dinner menu that evening included rice. Not rice and gravy. Not rice and beans. Not even rice and a rusty can of something at the bottom of the cabinet. Plain. White. Rice. My sister-in-law, Onaleah, was prepping her two ingredients (rice and water) when Bill looked out the window and saw a much better dinner staring back at him. Right about then, that rabbit would have been much safer playing in rush-hour traffic.

Now, some of you may wonder: Was it hunting season? Was this during daylight hours? Were they outside the city limits? Was the trailer in an isolated section of the park? Again, if you knew Bill, you'd know that the answer to all of the above is that he didn't care, not even a little bit. At that moment, all that mattered was whether he could scrounge up a cartridge for his .22 rifle. And he did. As my sister-in-law tells it, less than an hour passed between the *pop* of a rifle in her yard and a plate of bones by her sink.

Some people say that the rabbit must have come straight from heaven. If that's the case, all I can say is that Bill sent him back before they ever knew he was gone.

Note: Illustration at the beginning of the chapter "Bounty of the Land." *Artist rendering by John Paul King.*

Part V

DADGUMMIT!

It's easy to watch professionals fishing and hunting on television and get the idea that every trip ends in success. They always kill the trophy buck or haul in a boatload of whatever fish they were after. It's the kind of thing that makes the uninitiated wonder what all the fuss is about.

But that's television. In real life, things tend to go wrong from time to time. Not everyone has brand-new gear, just the right guns or expensive tackle. Some of us have to make do with what we have. And sometimes we make decisions that we look back on as questionable at best.

That's especially true in rural Northwest Florida, where most of us take pride in being able to use our ingenuity to overcome our lack of sophisticated equipment. Sometimes that works out in our favor. Other times it doesn't.

DREAMS OF STUFF THAT WORKS

Every time there's a huge lottery or Powerball jackpot, people talk about what they would do with all that money if they won. Mostly it's the same old stuff—mansions, vacation homes, yachts, expensive cars and the like. Not

Sunken steamship. *Courtesy of State Archives of Florida, Florida Memory, http://floridamemory.com/iems/show/28176.*

me, though. My dreams are much simpler. I have enough stuff. I just want stuff that works like it's supposed to.

I could list two dozen things I own that function just well enough to keep me from taking them to the dump but not well enough to count on at any given time. Why? I suspect it's a genetic condition or a curse handed down through the generations. One thing I'm sure of is that I got it from my father.

Most kids learn from their dads how to maintain things like cars, boats, lawn mowers and so on. If you grew up with Gene McClellan, however, the most frequent lessons focused on jury-rigging whatever you were using just long enough to get the job done. And if you were using his stuff, that knowledge was incredibly handy.

For example, Bill and I were driving Daddy's old '72 Bronco to the camp one day when we heard something dragging on the ground. We thought it might be the muffler, but when we looked under the truck, we discovered that, nope, it was the gas tank. The metal straps had rusted apart, and the tank was scraping along the road.

Broken trailer axle. *Photo by author.*

We found some rope, tied the tank back up to the body and went on our merry way. Bill told Daddy what happened, and he said, "Yep, I need to have that fixed." But two years later, when he traded the Bronco in for a new model, I saw the old one at the Chevrolet place downtown. Just for grins, I looked underneath. Sure enough, the same two pieces of rope were still there.

Throughout my childhood, I thought stuff like that was normal. It wasn't until later that I realized that other folks actually bought quality stuff, took care of it and counted on it to work when they needed it. The very next thing I realized is that quality stuff costs money, which is why Daddy often bought things that were past their prime. Preventive maintenance would be throwing good money after bad.

I'd like to say I learned from that experience, but a quick inventory around my house suggests otherwise. I have an ancient Evinrude outboard that Bill gave me. It's so old that I have to buy parts on the Internet. The mechanics have all but pronounced it dead, but I keep using it anyway. (Hey, it was free.)

My '98 Ford truck leaks when it rains, uses a quart of oil every thousand miles or so and the third door won't open. The lights on my trailer work about as well and as often as Congress. And most of my fishing rods are cut six inches shorter because the original tips have been broken off. But I'll keep patching them up to get as much use out of them as possible. That's because there was another lesson that Daddy taught me, though maybe not on purpose, that's just as significant. It's that things aren't nearly as important as experiences.

Daddy owned a lot of junk, but there are a lot of wealthy people in this world who didn't have nearly as much fun with a lot nicer boats, trucks and guns. It's true that money doesn't buy happiness, so I'm not waiting on wealth to start enjoying life. If I ever do strike it rich, however, you can bet I'll have stuff that works.

THE OLD JOHNSON OUTBOARD

One of the many characters who shaped my early life was my father's younger brother (and polar opposite), Billy McClellan. In his life, Uncle Billy had many occupations, ranging from submarine sailor to schoolteacher to game warden. He was licensed to fly planes, pilot tugboats and drive semi-trucks. Before he passed away in 1999, he had raced boats and cars and crossed both the Equator and the Arctic Circle.

He was good at anything mechanical, but there was one field in which he was more than merely gifted and, in fact, approached savant levels of genius. Uncle Billy may have been the best outboard motor mechanic who ever turned a wrench. He had an intuitive understanding of motors and machines, and watching him open a hood or remove a cowling was like seeing Chet Atkins pick up a guitar. It was second nature, as was his inclination to help anyone who needed it.

I was the beneficiary of his generous nature on a number of occasions, including once while I was off at basic training. I left my old, raggedy Ford truck parked at my parents' house for about four months. It wasn't in good shape to begin with, and after sitting idle for so long, I wondered if it would even crank. But when I got home, my father told me that Uncle Billy had used my truck a couple of times while I was away. That was terrific news because it was beyond his ability to notice a problem and not fix it. Sure enough, I came back to a truck that was running far better than it ever had.

However, Uncle Billy performed his most memorable mechanical miracle several years before then, when I was about ten years old. And I don't know if he ever realized what an indelible impact it made on my life.

It started with a 1959 3.5-horsepower Johnson outboard that had been sitting in my father's shed for as long as I could remember. It was old and rusted, and several pieces had been removed and scattered around in various places. For some reason, however, I decided that the old motor should be mine. I spent hours fantasizing about driving it down Iamonia Lake (on my imaginary boat, apparently). All I needed was someone to help me get it running.

Daddy said I could have the old motor, probably figuring that would be the end of it. However, he underestimated my determination to have it running again and apparently forgot how much his younger brother loved a mechanical challenge. I made an impassioned plea to Uncle Billy, who readily agreed to get it running again, but only if I helped. What happened next is the reason why God created summer breaks.

Home from his tugboat duties for a few days, Uncle Billy and I took the motor over to his house and began the meticulous process of tearing it down, piece by piece. With his toolbox, a pad and paper and a washtub with diesel fuel, we stripped the motor down to its smallest constituent pieces. All the while, he was making careful notes about what needed to be replaced. In the process, Uncle Billy explained to me in painstaking detail how an internal combustion engine works, the unique way an outboard operates and why some pieces had to be scrapped while others could be salvaged.

After we had the motor disassembled, Uncle Billy had to go back to work on the tugboat. While he was gone, my job was to take each part and clean it thoroughly with diesel fuel. Tibetan monks would have envied my complete devotion to this task. Every day, I walked over to his house and diligently cleaned each piece, being especially careful not to lose a nut, bolt or screw.

My other job was to approach my father about the delicate issue of ordering parts. Uncle Billy had made a list of all the things we needed and priced them in a catalogue at the old Chevrolet dealership (which also sold Johnson outboards because this was Blountstown and that's how we rolled). He estimated it was going to cost about thirty to forty dollars, and he wanted to make sure his notoriously cheap older brother was willing to pick up the tab.

So, I worked up the courage to approach Daddy and ask him if it would be okay to order the parts, offering to do odd jobs around the house to work off the bill and…Nah, just kidding. That's what I *should* have done. What I *really* did was lie through my teeth.

Having that motor was way too important to me to take a chance on Daddy saying no. So, I told Uncle Billy that Daddy had approved the purchase, and he went ahead and ordered the parts. I was counting on having the motor repaired and running before he got the bill. (Strategic miscalculations like that have been a hallmark of my life and career.)

It didn't pan out that way because Daddy came home at lunch one day and patiently explained why what I did was wrong, forgave me and left me with a big hug…Nah, just kidding. He hit the roof and threatened to take forty dollars worth of value off my backside if I ever pulled something like that again. But he also said he couldn't send the parts back and had to go ahead and pay for them, so we might as well finish the job. (This was an early lesson in asking forgiveness before permission that has actually served me quite well over the years.)

Waiting for Uncle Billy to get back off the tugboat was like waiting for Christmas to come. Every day, I scrubbed parts. Then I would wipe them down and scrub them some more. My biggest fear during this time was that it wasn't going to be good enough and thus would delay the day when I finally got to drive my own motor.

After what seemed like a month of waiting, Uncle Billy finally returned from his two-week stint and called me over to reassemble the motor. I remember laying newspapers out on the floor and then spreading the parts out all across the living room. Aunt Ann had no doubt surrendered her living room to this sort of thing before because she was a lot more tolerant than any other woman I've known before or since. She simply walked around us, unfazed by the fact that we had turned her home into a makeshift garage.

Piece by piece and part by part, we gradually put it all back together. Once again, Uncle Billy explained what each component did and why it was necessary. To me, it was complex and fascinating, but to a man who had repaired, overhauled and raced some of the largest outboards in production, I'm pretty sure it was less difficult than changing a tire.

As we were putting the final parts together, it was getting close to 9:00 p.m., and my brother Bill showed up to bring me home. I distinctly remember two things about what happened next. First, Bill made the comment that the old motor would never crank. He said that there was no way it could sit up that long and be resurrected with a few new parts and some TLC.

The next thing I remember is Uncle Billy smiling as he put the motor in a barrel and yanked the cord. On the first try, nothing happened. Second try, still nothing. But on the third pull, that old motor came to life, purring and putting like new.

The sight of that motor running filled my heart with joy and my mind with possibilities. I could tell my buddies—honestly—that I now had my own outboard motor. (A big deal for a kid back then.) It was a step toward manhood. It was independence. It was redemption. But mostly, it was mine.

Of course, I thanked Uncle Billy profusely, and I know he was proud of once again seeing a broken, neglected engine return to service.

Uncle Billy passed away in 1999, and I tried to make it over to see him one last time, but he died while I was en route. And though I'm usually at a loss for words in situations like that, I knew exactly what I wanted to say to him before he left us: Thanks for taking the time to bring a young boy's dream to life before his eyes and for teaching him what's possible with a skilled hand, a sharp mind and a patient heart.

It Tastes Nothing Like Chicken

My father-in-law was complaining one evening about raccoons, debating the best way to keep them out of his garbage cans. He didn't mind them visiting his yard or scrounging for food. His biggest complaint about them was the mess they left. "They got into some Styrofoam containers, tore them to pieces and left them all over the yard," he said. "I don't know why they can't just eat the food without scattering trash everywhere."

I offered up my all-purpose, go-to solution that involves a spotlight, a .22 rifle and neighbors who mind their own business. He speculated that the best thing to do would be to kill one and leave its carcass in the yard as a warning for others. However, my mother-in-law vetoed that idea pretty quickly.

As we were having this conversation (over dinner), it reminded me of the first raccoon I ever killed. It happened when I was about nine years old. I'm not sure which one of my brothers was involved, but whichever it was saw a 'coon up in the highest branches of a hickory tree. Nothing would do but for me to shoot him with my old single-shot twenty-gauge. It took two blasts of no. 8s, but after the second one, he tumbled to the ground with a *thud*.

As luck would have it, my father was barbecuing chicken at the Iamonia Lake Clubhouse that day and had told us to stop by for lunch after we were done hunting. That was perfect because it meant I'd get to show off my trophy to him and all the other folks who were gathered there. (It's hard to overestimate how important that last part was to a young boy.)

When we got there, I dragged the 'coon up to the old cinderblock and steel grill on the side of the Clubhouse to show my father. Daddy smiled and said, "Good job" or something. But since he was busy cooking, Charlie Cook Bridges offered to show me how to skin the thing out. Very shortly, I had my very own raccoon hide, ready to be tanned and hung on the wall.

I brought the hide back to show Daddy, but all he said was, "Where's the rest of him?" I explained that I threw the carcass into the creek.

"Go get it and finish cleaning him," he said. All of a sudden, I didn't like where this was going. I waded into the creek, got the earthly remains of my 'coon and cleaned him as well as a nine-year-old is inclined to do. I brought it back over to my father and watched as he quartered the carcass and threw it on the grill.

I remember thinking, "Who in the world is going to eat that with all this delicious chicken sitting here?" I learned the answer as soon as I grabbed a plate and reached for that very chicken.

"Oh no you don't," Daddy said, pointing at the 'coon. "You're not eating chicken. Your lunch is right over there." While everyone else got a plate of slow-cooked barbecue leg quarters, I had to wait on old, boar 'coon to go from raw to rare. When it looked done enough, Daddy slathered some barbecue sauce on it, turned it a couple of times and then slapped it on my plate. I ate as much of the meat as I could, but I couldn't stand it and made another run at the chicken.

"What's the matter? You didn't like that 'coon?" Daddy asked.

"No, sir."

"Well, too bad. Next time, don't shoot one unless you plan on eating it or you know somebody who will."

From that day until this one, every raccoon I see brings back memories of pink, musky meat, covered in barbecue sauce with a lead pellet in every other bite. I've ignored a lot of my father's advice over the years, but no matter what else I've done, you can bet I never shot another 'coon.

THE CHIPOLA FROG ODYSSEY

Chipola College in Marianna, Florida, takes its name from the Chipola River, which originates nearby. This is a story about the incredible talent it takes to get into trouble in both of those places at the same time.

Our adventure started late one night during finals week, a time when all the students were busy preparing for the exams that could make or break their GPA. All the students except for two, that is. My friend Gary Wayne Purvis and I had decided on a bolder, more practical approach to preparing for the end of the term.

By the end of the spring semester in 1984, we knew our only hope for passing was divine intervention, major computer errors or the apocalypse. (And we would have gladly accepted any of them.) So, using the same sound judgment that had gotten us in this pickle to begin with, we came up with a brilliant plan to soften the blow when our parents got our grades.

Knowing how much our fathers loved eating frog legs, we decided it would be better to hunt for frogs to use as a peace offering than to study for tests we weren't going to pass anyway. (It was the kind of logic that only eighteen-year-old boys fully understand.)

We met up with another friend named Emory Godwin around 10:00 p.m. and headed down the Chipola River on GW's boat. My father was asleep in front of the television as I was leaving, so I nudged him and let him know where I was going. He mumbled something unintelligible that I interpreted as, "Fine. Be careful."

An hour or so later, the three of us—GW, Emory and I—had made our way a few miles downstream to the mouth of the Old River, a small oxbow off the Chipola. Once we got there, however, we found that the water was only about six inches deep for a distance of twenty to thirty feet. That meant we had to get out of the boat and pull it across the shallow entrance and into the deeper water on the other side. That effort paid off big because the place turned out to be an amphibian goldmine. By the time we made a second pass, we had an ice chest full of frogs and were ready to head home.

Small bullfrog on a tree root. *Photo by Domenick Esgro,* Calhoun-Liberty Journal.

Everybody knows it's trouble when a redneck says, "Boys, watch this!" Well, here's another phrase that should raise a red flag: anything that includes the words "let's get a running start." If you hear either of those things, nothing good is going to happen next.

Sure enough, on the way back, Gary Wayne decided that we didn't need to get out and wade across the sand and gravel barrier. Instead, we would hit it at full speed in his welded-aluminum boat and blast our way through. After all, boats like his were built to take that kind of punishment.

To Gary Wayne's credit—and my great surprise—we actually made it. Of course, it happened with all the grace and half the noise of a major train wreck. GW was in my lap, I was in shock and Emory was in pain on the deck. But we did make it. It was only when we started upriver that we realized there was a major problem.

Unlike his boat, it turns out that Gary Wayne's outboard was not built to plow through several yards of river bottom. (Who woulda thunk it?) The motor was running, but the prop looked like somebody had run a beer can through a blender. One blade was gone completely, one was broken in half and the other was bent beyond recognition.

They say it's bad to be "up the creek without a paddle." I can tell you firsthand that it's worse to be down the river without a propeller. There was no way we would be able to paddle that heavy boat three miles upstream to the landing. And at the speed we were drifting, it would be a few hours before we reached anything downriver.

Along about 1:00 a.m., though, we drifted up close to Jehue Landing and decided that our best option was to land the boat there and walk. What followed was the kind of journey that inspires epic poems, Bible stories and Disney movies.

Jehue was a couple of miles past nowhere. So our original plan was to knock on the door of the first house we came to. However, a couple of pit bulls explained to us in dog terms that we probably shouldn't do that. Plus, in Calhoun County, showing up on a stranger's porch in the middle of the night is still a really good way to get shot. If we were going to get home in one piece, it was clear we were going to do it on foot.

So, we soldiered on for about six miles—across soybean fields, through briar patches and along dim roads. I had sprained my ankle not long before, and Emory's knee was giving him trouble, so our long walk was really a series of short, painful hikes between rest stops. I've seen old people shuffle through buffet lines faster than we were going.

About dawn, we finally reached an old trailer owned by Gary Wayne's family. There, we broke into his Uncle Mike's Jeep and drove it back to GW's house. His mother, Susan, greeted us with all the warmth she could muster for three sweaty, frog-smelling guys at 6:00 a.m.

One of my biggest worries at that point was the possibility that my father might have search parties looking for us. I could picture him being both concerned and mad. But mostly mad. I was sweating bullets when I called home.

"I just want to let you know I'm all right," I said when he answered the phone. "We just had some problems with the boat, but I'll be home in a few minutes."

His response was touching: "Oh, I forgot you were gone." And when I told him what happened, his only comment reflected all the sympathy and concern I had come to expect through the years: "Well, did you get any frogs?"

For his part, GW did manage to swing an A in archery class, which he tried to portray as the silver lining to a very dark cloud. His dad, a shrewd judge of the job market, was unimpressed. "There's not much need for a modern-day Robin Hood," Big Gary said. It could have been worse, though. The only A on my report card was the one in my last name.

But while we might not have knocked the top out of our classes at Chipola, nobody can say we didn't get an education while we were there.

THE GREAT CANOE RACE

On a hot August night in 1985, I answered the phone, and the first words I heard on the other end were, "You've got to wax the bottom of the canoe." It was my friend Shawn Wood, who, along with Jerry Peacock, Jamie Maupin and me, was competing in a Marianna–Blountstown canoe race down the Chipola River the following day.

The fact that we knew almost nothing about canoes didn't keep us from signing up for the race. And, as evidenced by Shawn's call, we actually thought we had a pretty good chance of winning. Later, we learned that the chances were just as good we'd be struck by lightning after hitting the lotto twice, but at nine o'clock the night before, it was still several hours before we would be dunked under the cold waters of reality. (That's a hint at how the rest of this story plays out.)

I don't know about the other three, but my first moment of doubt came at the launch, when I stepped into the borrowed canoe and almost fell out before it was all the way in the water. Lined up beside us were several people we didn't know, some of whom looked like professional canoe racers. They had sleek new boats and curved paddles, and as soon as the gun sounded, they left our sight forever.

Jerry and I were left behind with Shawn and Jamie, all struggling to find our rhythm. The only canoe behind us held Ginny and Clay Knight, who were fully involved in a sibling argument that started before the race and (I'm told) lasted well after it was done.

Despite their freshly waxed canoe, Shawn and Jamie fell behind as we finally got our act together and headed south. We had only made it about two bends downstream when we saw a hornets' nest hanging low over the river. What happened next is a matter of debate, but what I remember (the truth) is that Jerry tried to steer us right (from the bow) while I tried to steer us left (from the stern). We ended up going straight (into the water).

We were soaked, and all our provisions for a day on the water (including our water) went straight to the bottom. Just when I thought it couldn't get worse, Shawn and Jamie came by, laughing hysterically. Karma, however, is a beautiful thing sometimes. Once we righted our canoe and got back in, we caught up with Shawn and Jamie just up the river, where they were stuck on a log under the middle of their boat. They were rocking furiously trying to get free.

Something had to give, and it did. Just as we passed, the old canoe cracked open on both sides. So, we stopped immediately and offered to provide whatever help we could. Yeah, right. What we actually did was point and laugh and keep paddling. We might have even splashed them on the way by…I don't really remember.

At one of the later checkpoints, we learned that Jamie had abandoned the broken canoe and caught a ride home. Shawn, on the other hand, was still in the race, last seen paddling a half-sunken boat.

Keep in mind that we were expecting to be in Blountstown by early afternoon, but we actually arrived about 7:30 or 8:00 p.m. The race was long over, the prizes had been awarded and the only two people left at the landing were Betsy Knight, waiting on Clay and Ginny, and Cheryl Wood, who was there to retrieve our crew.

After half an hour or so, only Shawn was still unaccounted for, and Cheryl, who had been there since God knows when, decided that we needed to find him. It didn't take long. After pulling up to a friend's camp, we heard a voice in the darkness—a familiar voice…singing. What I saw next is hard to describe with mere words. Picture an upside-down canoe floating downriver, almost completely submerged, with Shawn spread out across the bottom, paddling with his hands and singing at the top of his lungs.

I'm only sorry that happened in the days before camera phones. I think it was Jerry who put into words what we were both thinking as Shawn drifted into the light: "Good thing you waxed the bottom of that canoe."

WATCH YOUR STEP

Raising five sons didn't make my father a great parent, at least not by the Ward Cleaver/Andy Griffith definition. But by the time I came along, his teaching methods had become incredibly efficient and brutally effective. For example, he understood that one moment of powerful or painful experience was worth hours of patient explanation. Anything that didn't kill us, maim us or damage his stuff was worth letting us learn on our own.

One such lesson that's fresh in my mind happened on a fishing trip when I was about eight or nine years old. Back then, Daddy kept an old wooden boat tied to the bank of the creek near our camp. During the spring and summer months, we often cooked and ate our catch right there. On those trips, my job was to lug all our poles, bait and other items down to the boat. Daddy's job was to supervise this process, make sure I didn't forget anything and provide an ongoing critique of whatever I was doing at the time.

This particular morning, as I hustled down the muddy creek bank with cane poles and the fish basket, I noticed that Daddy was watching me more closely than usual. When I dropped off my first load, he immediately sent me to the truck to get a couple more things. On the way back, he was watching me even more intently than before. No sooner had I gotten to the boat than he sent me to the truck again, this time for stuff I could have easily carried on the last trip. I mumbled futile complaints all the way there and back.

I had retrieved whatever he sent me for, but when I started to get in the boat, he said, "Stop right there, turn around and look back where you came from." Now I was mad. If I had dropped something, why didn't he just tell me then? Or better yet, why not go pick it up himself? (Being a parent, I now understand the reason behind the latter.) "See anything unusual?" he asked. Of course I didn't and said so. "Look at your footprints," he said. "You don't notice anything out of the ordinary?" All I saw was leaf litter and limbs, dotted by the bare mud where I had stepped. At this point, Daddy's tone grew more agitated. "Look right there!" he said, pointing to a grayish-brown limb in my path.

As I looked at the limb, I noticed it was looking back at me. "That's unusual," I thought. "Limbs don't normally…oh!" There—with three sets of my footprints on either side of him—was a four-foot-long white oak snake lying dead still, perfectly camouflaged by his surroundings. I had an instant, full-blown attack of the heebie-jeebies.

"Son, if that had been a moccasin, he would have struck you as soon as you got too close," Daddy said. "You'd better learn to watch where you're walking when you're in the woods." With that as a foundation, Daddy spent our time on the boat explaining which snakes were poisonous, where they liked to hide out and why you step on top of a log before you step over it. To his credit, I was a very receptive audience at that point.

Fast-forward a few decades. I was walking up a two-trail road near the very spot where I had met the white oak snake years before. I was focused on a clearing ahead, hoping to catch a turkey off guard. As intent as I was on killing a gobbler, I still managed a glance down at the road every now and then. And it's a good thing I did. Just as I was getting near the clearing, a small pile of leaves in front of my right foot morphed into a young gold-and-brown copperhead, nearly invisible but already half-coiled and ready to strike. I took a step back, regained my composure and then walked around him. I was a little shaken but also grateful for my father's lesson from nearly forty years earlier.

That experience has saved me a world of hurt lots of times since then. It's also made me realize that Daddy never worried about what anybody thought of his parenting methods. What he did care about was making sure his five boys could survive their own carelessness.

As it turns out, that alone was a pretty tough job.

GET YOUR KNIFE

I'm sure we all remember things we hated hearing our parents say—things like, "take out the trash," "mow the grass," "sit up straight," "don't scratch yourself in church" and "stop peeing in the yard." (Okay, those last two are things my wife says. But you get the point.) As a youngster, what I dreaded most was hearing my father say, "Get your knife and come here." That would put a baseball-sized knot in my stomach every time.

First, there was the problem that I never had my knife with me. This was inconceivable to my father because a pocketknife was an essential part of his being, like his wallet and wedding ring—or, more accurately, his ring finger. He just expected everyone to have a knife at all times.

When he told me to go get mine, it would cause a mad scramble as I tried to remember when and where I used it last. Assuming I found it, that just led to the next problem: my knife was always dull. Daddy would feel the blade, shake his head and tell me to sharpen it on his old whet rock. That usually worked about as well as giving a calculator to a chimpanzee and telling him to do your taxes. I still don't understand how my father could turn his old Case into a razor with about three strokes on the stone. Even now, I can use the same tools and technique and, if I'm not careful, turn mine into a butter knife.

But it didn't matter how sharp or dull it was because I'd still have to do whatever it was I needed the knife for in the first place. At best, it would be something simple like peeling onions or potatoes or cutting the stems off figs. But if he drove up with his boat in tow, it was a safe bet that he had a mess of fish, still in their natural state.

For my father, the number of fish that constituted a "mess" depended entirely on who was going to clean them. If one or more of his sons was at

Years after he passed away, my father's knife (left) remained as sharp as my brother's. *Photo by Bill McClellan.*

home, a mess was as many as he could catch before running out of daylight or bait, plus any that his buddies might give him along the way. Bringing back a basket with fifty to one hundred bream and shellcracker was pretty common.

Another, equally unattractive possibility was that he had shot a deer, one or more hogs, doves, ducks, squirrels, quail or any combination thereof. Being edible and available was a deadly combination for critters that crossed my father's path.

No matter what he brought home, it usually meant I was going to spend an hour or two with my hands in fur, feathers, scales, guts and/or blood. If I had a date that night, too bad. An acid bath and a vat of Old Spice wouldn't get rid of the smell. (Imagine what a confidence booster that was!)

When Daddy passed away in 2002, my mother gave me four or five of his old pocketknives. For sentimental reasons, I gave a couple of the knives to my son. It would come as no surprise to my father that his grandson now has no idea where those knives are today. But Daddy didn't attach a lot of sentimental value to things like knives. Instead, he would probably just take Jimmy to the hardware store and buy a new one, while telling him to keep up with his stuff. Or, more likely, he would tell me to give him one of mine. And I would gladly do that, except I don't know where any of them are right now.

That part wouldn't surprise him either.

LAZARUS THE REDFISH

I can't come up with a single story from our past that makes us look like anything other than potential Darwin Award candidates.
—Lee Kissell, reflecting on adventures from our younger days

It's rare when you can reduce a decades-long friendship to one simple sentence, but Lee pretty much summed up ours with that one. There's a fine line between careless and reckless. Between '85 and '90, he and I didn't just cross that line; there were several times when we built a ramp, got a running start and jumped way over to the other side.

Lee reminded me of one such incident from our misspent youth that involved a redfish caught at St. George Island. In all honesty, though, I lay a lot of blame for this one on New Orleans chef Paul Prudhomme. Thanks to that fat, fuzzy Cajun, the world's supply of redfish went from plentiful to "blackened" almost overnight.

As a result, Florida's Marine Fisheries Commission stepped in and for a few years made it illegal to keep even one redfish. Turns out that was a smart move. It only took a little while for the stocks to recover. But it took a few years before the state loosened up its rules on keeping them.

It was during that interim that Lee and I bought a boat and began fishing the coast like it was our job. (If I'm exaggerating, it's only because back then we didn't take our jobs quite as seriously as our fishing.) Of course, the redfish ban ensured that it was the only species we caught from then on, especially when we fished Bob Sikes Cut.

We released every redfish we caught, coming back empty-handed most days. After a while, it became a joke: the most expensive part of fishing was stopping by the seafood store on the way home. On one of these trips, we said enough was enough. So, we decided to tempt fate and slip one in the ice chest. (Side note: Fate doesn't resist temptation very well.)

Part of our rationale was that any fish we could catch consistently must be doing well. In fact, if we were catching them at all, it probably meant they were on the verge of overpopulation. Hell, we were likely doing the world a service by keeping one. A more important factor in this decision was that we had never seen a marine patrol officer in all the times we had fished the cut. (This is a literary device known as "foreshadowing.")

Our "illegal harvest" had been on ice for all of about fifteen minutes before a gray-and-black boat with blue lights appeared in the cut about one hundred yards away. It was the marine patrol. That meant the four-pound redfish in the cooler was now a $500 fine just waiting to be discovered. There was nowhere to run or hide as the big boat headed directly toward us. I could feel the color draining from my face and money I didn't have draining from my wallet.

But just as the officers had cut the distance between us in half, they turned ninety degrees right and pulled up to check the only other boat on our side of the cut. It was just the break we needed. Although they were close enough to clearly see what we were up to, both officers turned their backs long enough for me to reach in the ice chest and quickly toss our contraband catch overboard.

I breathed a sigh of relief, but it was cut short because of two troublesome developments: first, after spending fifteen minutes on ice, our redfish wasn't exactly an enthusiastic swimmer. Instead, he was a big, copper-colored carcass of state's evidence drifting in the current.

Second, said current was taking him on a beeline to the marine patrol boat just a few yards away.

I've yet to meet anyone who actually hoped a big one would get away, but that's exactly what we were doing at that moment. No one outside SeaWorld has ever been so focused on the health of a fish. "Come on, buddy!" we were saying. "You can make it. Please. Do it for your grandfish!"

As he bobbed downstream, I quietly considered testifying against Lee in exchange for leniency. But just seconds before the redfish became Exhibit A in *People v. Us*, he swirled his tail and dove below the surface, out of sight. He may be the only fish in history that was wished back to life.

As it turned out, all our worry was unnecessary. The officers cranked up their boat and went back the same way they came. By then, Lee and I were emotionally drained and ready to call it a day. So, we pulled up the anchor and headed for the landing. We did drive a little slower than usual, however. And we watched the water carefully—you know, just in case a half-frozen, brain-damaged redfish happened to pop up in front of us.

Learning from mistakes was never our strong suit.

LESSONS FROM A GASKIN STREET 'POSSUM WAR

I was in my twenties, I think, when I first learned that "discharging a firearm within the city limits" is a crime in many places. When I was growing up in Blountstown, it was sometimes a necessity and sometimes entertainment. And on rare occasions, it was both.

For example, during my senior year of high school, we had a pretty serious 'possum infestation around the house. That bothered my father because he worried that they would get into the attic or take up under the house. It bothered my mother because she flat-out hated 'possums. To her, they were hideous, giant rats with snakes for tails. Just the sight of one through the window would send her scrambling into the next room.

The solution was obvious: we just needed to relocate them to a more appropriate habitat. And by "relocate," I mean shoot. And by "appropriate habitat" I mean a hole in the backyard. Toward that end, Daddy brought out his old .22 rifle and propped it up beside the back door.

"If one of those 'possums wanders up, shoot him," Daddy said. That was all I needed to hear. With those words, Daddy had just opened hunting season in August, and I wasn't about to pass up the action. I'm sure he only meant for me to shoot a 'possum if I happened to see one in the course of my normal routine, but I decided to be more proactive. I actually set out a can of tuna on the patio and watched the backyard like it was a food plot.

The first night, I stayed up until 1:00 a.m., but the 'possums didn't show. The second night, one wandered up but ran off before I could get the door open. On night three, I managed to get the door open and fire off a shot, but I couldn't see the sights. Next night, same thing. There just wasn't enough contrast between the iron sights and the darkness of the night. By the fifth night, I decided to kick it up a notch. After my parents went to bed, I broke out the Remington 1100, loaded it up with no. 6s and started my nightly vigil.

It was after midnight when the 'possum waddled up on the porch, wearing his smug 'possum grin and dragging his snake-tail behind him. I slid the glass door open as fast as I could and shot twice, the second just for good measure. Two spent shells lay on the floor, and the smell of cordite was thick in the air. The 'possum war was over, at least for now, and I took pride in knowing I had repelled the invasion.

Right about then, I heard Daddy's feet hit the floor and come bounding toward the kitchen. I'm sure I had a grin on my face when he rounded the corner, bleary-eyed and highly agitated. "What are you doing?!" he asked in a rather loud tone.

"I shot the 'possum," I said proudly.

Instead of thanking me for defending our homestead, he just growled, "You can't fire off a twelve-gauge in the backyard in the middle of town. You probably woke up everybody on Gaskin Street." As if on cue, the phone rang, and Daddy answered. It was Mrs. Kathryn Tucker next door.

"Yeah, we're okay…no, he was just shooting a 'possum…sorry about that…you too." As soon as he hung up, it rang again. This time, it was the same conversation with Earl Dority, who lived across the street. After another call or two, Daddy finished his tirade and stormed back to bed. I'm not sure what lesson he intended to leave me with, but I went away with the understanding that it was perfectly fine to shoot a rimfire in town but not a shotgun because it makes too much noise.

Years later, I read a newspaper story about a man who was arrested in some town up north for using a twelve-gauge to shoot mistletoe out of a tree. I remember shaking my head and thinking, "Of course he got arrested. Probably disturbed the whole neighborhood. Should have used a .22 like you're supposed to."

Note: Illustration at the beginning of the chapter "Bad Day on the Water." *Artist rendering by John Paul King.*

Part VI

TO SAVE A RIVER

There's a stand of willows at the south end of Iamonia Lake, right in the middle of the channel. If you're driving your boat on that stretch, you have to choose right or left. One way takes you to the river; the other leads you to a shallow, muddy dead end.

There's nothing special about this willow island, except that it wasn't there back in the '70s. The water was too high. When I was growing up, you could run a boat wide open on a straight shot down the lake and out into the Apalachicola. Not anymore. Now we have to choose our path.

Unfortunately, Iamonia Lake is just one symptom of a problem that plagues the Apalachicola in its entirety. Once navigable sloughs, lakes and ponds now are dry or extremely low for much of the year. I can hunt in some of the same places where I used to catch fish. I can see the dry white sand and loose pebbles where I know the bream and shellcracker would bed if only there was water.

For several years now, people have been pointing to troubling signs like lower-than-usual water levels lasting longer than ever before. I've spoken to people in their sixties, seventies and eighties who say they've never seen it this low this long. Creeks have turned into footpaths. Ponds are indistinguishable from the surrounding woods. Cypress trees are struggling to survive, sometimes now hundreds of feet from water.

Florida, Alabama and Georgia are locked in a three-way battle for their fair share of the water. Georgia wants to feed the ever-growing beast that is Atlanta. Alabama wants to make sure there's enough left to water its crops. And the folks at Lake Seminole don't want their slice of heaven to go to hell in a handbasket.

With heavy development in Miami, Orlando and Tampa, people in the Panhandle long anticipated a north-versus-south battle over water. We just didn't realize we would be the south—the downstream side of an uphill fight to preserve the Apalachicola. At stake here is nothing less than our way of life, our recreational opportunities and the measure of self-sufficiency that hunting and fishing make possible.

All of us in the tri-state area have a lot to lose, and I get that. But I wonder if the people in Georgia and Alabama understand that what we have south of the Jim Woodruff Dam is a river system that can never be rebuilt or replanted. We can't develop a new tributary like we create a suburban neighborhood. We can't rotate the "crops" of cypress, tupelo, white oak and hickory trees along its course—much less the fish and oysters in the bay. And we can't engineer a state-of-the-art swamp somewhere else.

My point is that folks to our north may have a lot at stake here, but we're "all in." Less water for them is inconvenient; for the Apalachicola River, it's catastrophic.

There was a time when the river could be all things to all people: a drinking water supply for our neighbors to the north, a transportation system linking the mountains to the sea and a source of recreation and sustenance for everyone fortunate enough to live along its path. That time has passed. Now we have to choose which of those things deserves our greatest efforts to protect. It's an important choice. One way can take us to a sustainable, healthy river system; the other will leave us high and dry.

Despite the well-documented problems, I'm optimistic about the future of the river. I believe that organizations like the Apalachicola Riverkeeper, talented artists like Elam Stoltzfus and Clyde Butcher and the people in communities up and down the river are having a positive impact and raising public awareness about the plight of the Apalachicola. Sooner or later, the people in all three states will come together and agree on the importance of saving it. When they do, the elected leaders will have no choice but to follow suit and take action.

For my part, I believe the most important role I can play in this effort is to continue writing about the wonders of the river and about the unique people who call the area home. I can remember the people who came before me and leave a record for those who will follow.

Headed upstream on the Apalachicola River. *Photo by Domenick Esgro,* Calhoun-Liberty Journal.

Most of all, I can still enjoy every day I get to spend on its waters, along its banks and in the areas nearby. And I intend to enjoy as many of those days as possible.

Note: Illustration at the beginning of the chapter "Peace Like a River." *Artist rendering by John Paul King.*

ABOUT THE AUTHOR AND ARTISTS

Jim McClellan is a fifth-generation Florida native from Blountstown who left the floodplains of the Apalachicola River and spent ten years in the even murkier waters of state government. A 1987 graduate of Florida State, Jim served as a speechwriter for Governor Lawton Chiles, communications director for the Florida Department of Commerce and press secretary for Lieutenant Governor Buddy MacKay. These days, Jim makes his home in Pensacola and makes his living doing marketing for an e-mail and web security company in Gulf Breeze. He's passionate about protecting and restoring the Apalachicola River and about preserving the traditions of hunting, fishing and outdoors living.

SUZANNE CONNER

I am incredibly grateful to Suzanne Foster Conner for her paintings that present the Apalachicola River and surrounding areas exactly the way they live in my memories. Her work captures perfectly what we both remember from our childhood along the river—a distant, magical time she describes as beautifully in print as she does in paint:

I am continually amazed at the raw beauty of the land and rivers where I was born and raised in Calhoun County, Florida. The Apalachicola River and the fertile grounds all around were our stomping grounds growing up for many wonderful adventures. We followed our grandfather Carey Yates all over the county, walking it, discovering Indian mounds, looking for wild violets and learning to respect this beautiful land that our Creator left for us to care for. It was at my grandfather's knee that we learned about finding water with divining rods and the excitement of hunting season and the good eating this land provided. This is what inspired me to leave a career of almost thirty years of decorating interiors to follow a passion of creating on canvas with paint. I have enjoyed working with the author, Jim McClellan, on this project since we both share a love and respect for this wonderful place we have called home, surrounding the mysterious and winding Apalachicola River.

Suzanne lives and paints in Tallahassee, with her husband, Bryant, and her daughter, Lindsey, nearby. You can see her artwork at suzanneconnerart.com and on her blog, fireflyevenings.com.

JOHN PAUL KING

Pensacola artist John Paul King is an artist whose talents span a number of media, from the pen-and-ink drawings seen at the beginning of each chapter to oil paintings to computer graphics to music. I'm fortunate that JP is also a friend, colleague and fellow outdoorsman who understands and appreciates the culture of self-reliance and subsistence that fuels my passion for hunting and fishing and other outdoor pursuits. With little beyond crude descriptions and timeworn photos to work from, JP has successfully resurrected scenes that now exist only in my memories. Other examples of JP's art can be found at johnpaulking.net.

www.ingramcontent.com/pod-product-compliance
Lightning Source LLC
Chambersburg PA
CBHW060814100426
42813CB00004B/1066